LECTURES

TO

YOUNG MEN.

By WILLIAM G. ELIOT, Jr.
PASTOR OF THE CHURCH OF THE MESSIAH, ST. LOUIS.

Seventh Edition.

BOSTON:
CROSBY, NICHOLS, AND COMPANY.
NEW YORK:
CHARLES S. FRANCIS AND COMPANY.
1858.

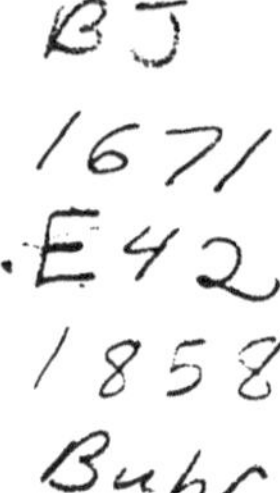

CAMBRIDGE:
METCALF AND COMPANY, STEREOTYPERS AND PRINTERS.

CONTENTS.

INTRODUCTORY LECTURE.

AN APPEAL.

"I have written unto you, young men, because ye are strong, and the word of God abideth in you, and ye have overcome the wicked one. Love not the world, neither the things that are in the world. If any man love the world, the love of the Father is not in him. For all that is in the world, the lust of the flesh, and the lust of the eyes, and the pride of life, is not of the Father, but is of the world. And the world passeth away, and the lust thereof: but he that doeth the will of God abideth for ever." — 1 John ii. 14–17.

I PROPOSE, as already announced, to give several discourses to young men, addressed to them as a distinct class in the community and as individuals. For such an undertaking we have the authority and example of an Apostle, who, in the words of my text, addresses his exhortations to young men, with a degree of solemnity that shows the importance attached to this part of his preaching. He repeats the same words twice, and with increasing emphasis: "I write unto you, young men, because ye have overcome the wicked one"; and again, "I have written unto you, young men, because ye are strong, and the word of God abideth in you, and ye have overcome the wicked one."

This apostolical example we would follow; this Scriptural authority we would use. I desire to address the young men of this society, and all those who are willing to hear me, in the words of soberness and truth. Under different circumstances and with a feebler tongue; but with a purpose I trust equally true, and with a work to be accomplished, not less important than that which the Apostles themselves were sent to accomplish. For their work was to speak in Christ's stead, persuading men to be reconciled to God; and the same work is committed to every minister of Christ, at the present day. They may do it badly; they may work as hirelings, and not as faithful shepherds; but their work, whether done or neglected, is the same.

The circumstances, however, under which the Apostle spoke are very different from our own. He addressed those only who were members of the Church of Christ, who had already made a good profession and proved their sincerity by lives of obedience. For he says, "I have written unto you, young men, because ye are strong"; that is, strong in the Lord and in the power of his might, "and the word of God abideth in you, and ye have overcome the wicked one." In that day there were very few nominal Christians. Those who bore the name of Christ were also compelled to bear his cross. They who came to hear Christian preaching carried their lives in their hands, and the young men of a Christian society were an army of self-devoted followers of Him, under whose standard they were enlisted. I wish that it were so now. The outward danger is past, but I wish that the self-devotion could continue.

Unhappily for the Christian cause, it is not so. Of all the young men in this city, who were educated by Christian parents, and who in common language would call themselves Christians, not one tenth have a full right to that name; not one tenth have so much as professed their faith in Christ. How small a number can be said to have a well-founded hope in him! In this society, there are probably two or three hundred young men; I mean that there is at least that number who make this their usual place of worship, when they attend church at all. How small a part of them take their place at the communion-table of Christ! or, to apply a more general test, how small a part of them can be said to have had a personal religious experience!

The majority of young men are unfixed in their religious opinions, irresolute in their religious purposes, irregular in their religious duties. Many of them are unsettled in their principles of conduct and have no fixed plan of life. They are floating upon the surface of society, carried one way or the other by the currents of social influence, by the changing wind of good or ill success. They are not strong; the word of God does not yet abide in them; they have not overcome the wicked one. They are trusting, it would seem, to the natural progress of things for their salvation, instead of working it out with fear and trembling.

Young men! I speak seriously and earnestly, but do I not speak truly? I would not bring an unjust charge, but I fear that there is something radically wrong, which needs to be corrected. The wrong may be in the speaker, more than the hearer; in the minister, more than in the people; for surely if religion were presented, as it ought to be, in its simplicity and power, there would not be so many of the young who turn away from it, with indifference or contempt. Our churches ought to be filled with young men. Our communion-table should be crowded with them; our Sunday school, our ministry to the poor, our Christian missions, and every religious enterprise, should be made prosperous by their coöperation; and this would be the case, if the Gospel of Christ were brought home to their hearts as it ought to be. That it is not done, is undoubtedly the fault of those to whom the dispensation of the Gospel is committed. If the truth could be preached as it is in Jesus, surely the young would hear it. Would to God that I could now speak so that every one who hears me would feel rebuked for his sinfulness, and go from this house with his heart full of that infinite question, "What shall I do to be saved?"

This is my reason for speaking so plainly; for in plainness of speech is my only hope of success. This is the cause of my anxiety; for while there are so many young men who show their confidence in me by making this the place of their worship, but to whom it is not made the savor of life unto life, there is reason to fear that my own duty is but imperfectly performed.

Do not understand me, however, as saying or thinking that the salvation of my hearers depends upon me. I abhor that arrogance of the priestly office, by which such claims are made, as though the minister, the servant of Christ, were the mediator between God and man. Nor can we excuse the worldly-minded and indifferent, as though they could plead, before the bar of God, the dulness or inefficiency of their religious teachers, in palliation of their sins. No: your souls are, under God, in your own keeping. With the Bible in your hands, you have no sufficient excuse for ignorance, nor worldliness, nor sin. With God's instructors all around you, and in your own hearts, you cannot plead the want of faithful teachers. With a mother's blessing resting upon your head, and the recollection of a mother's words rising unbidden in your hearts, you cannot plead the want of motive to lead a pure and religious life.

The ultimate responsibility, therefore, must rest with yourselves, even with each one of you. Nevertheless, when we look around upon the multitude of young men with whom this city is filled, and the evil influences to which they are exposed; when we see how large a part of them are walking in the broad but dangerous road that leads to destruction, and how few, comparatively, are even seeking for the way of eternal life, we cannot help feeling that every one who occupies a Christian pulpit has a duty to fulfil towards them, which has not yet been perfectly accomplished.

It would be unjust to say that the young men of St. Louis, compared with those of other cities, are below the general standard. I have no sufficient means for making such a comparison, but think that, if it were fairly made, the judgment would not be against us. The average degree of morality and of respect for religion is perhaps as high here as elsewhere. When all the circumstances are considered, it is higher than could have been reasonably expected; but no one will deny that there is great room for improvement. The standard even of common morality among our young men is not so high as it ought to be, and religion is too little regarded. We need some new element at work among them; we need some stronger influence to counteract the worldly and irreligious influences by which they are surrounded.

Look at their numbers. A gray-haired man is but now and then seen among us. See how early they enter upon the active duties of life.

At the age of fifteen or sixteen, they are found in their places of business doing their part, and before ten years are past, they have become the merchants and enterprising men of the city. Take away from our city the young men, and how little would be left of all its present vigor and enterprise! There is no city of the world, probably, in which young men occupy a more important position; none in which a greater responsibility, for good or evil, rests upon them. Do they feel this as they ought? Do they understand the greatness of their work, and the importance of doing it well and quickly?

It is perceived in part, but not as it ought to be. There are some who feel it, but there are still more who think only of the fortune they have come to seek, and of the pleasures they pursue. The cause of religion and of morality, the moral interests of society, the progress of truth and goodness, give them no concern. If they can obtain the means of living, and have enough to spare for their amusements, their work is accomplished: and in the choice of their amusements they are guided, not by their sense of what is right and wrong, but by considerations of convenience and of custom. What others do, they will do; where others go, they will go. The degree of decency or respectability required by the circle in which they move, they will try to attain, and if they do not sink much below it, they are content. Thus evil customs prevail more and more; thus the tendency with so many is continually downwards. Thus it happens, that hundreds of those who come here with general intentions of living a good life, breathe an impure atmosphere and become morally tainted from the very first. Thus it is, that so many run a rapid career, through frivolity and self-indulgence and sin, ending in contempt and ruin.

Go through our city from one end to the other, through its principal streets and sub urbs, on the week-day and on the Sabbath We do not ask you to look upon the low haunts of vice, the dens of vile iniquity, whose secrets you may not even think upon without the stain of impurity; but look at the more respectable places of resort, where the cup of pleasure is made to sparkle, and the appliances of luxury are used to introduce the appliances of vice. Look in, — you need not enter, — look in upon the splendid rooms appropriated exclusively to tippling and games of chance. Consider what enormous profits must accrue from such establishments, and ask yourselves BY WHOM they are chiefly supported. I would speak diffidently upon subjects on which I am unavoidably to a great extent ignorant. We know that those doors are darkened, too often, by the forms of men, whose proper place is with their wives and their children, and even with their children's children, at their own homes. A heavy guilt do they incur, who, with the soberness of years resting upon them and the serious duties of mature life to discharge, yet give their countenance to the dram-shop,—for that is its name be it ever so splendid, — and their influence to the cause of dissipation and sin. But their number I would fain believe is small.

If I may trust my own observation and what is told me by others, the chief responsibility for the growth of intemperance and other forms of vice among us rests upon the young themselves; upon young men, who are betrayed into habits which at first seem only foolish, but which by rapid growth become sinful, because they think that youth will excuse them, and that while young they have a right to do as they please. Beginning with occasional indulgence, feeling that they are unobserved, or that what they do is of no importance one way or the other, they gradually form habits which place them among the opponents of virtue and the devotees of sin. Sometimes they stop before it is too late, and with saddened hearts begin a life of sobriety and usefulness. But even then, ought they not to consider that they have been doing an incalculable harm to the cause of sound morality and religion; that they have been lending their influence to the support of institutions which are the curse of our community?

This is the first ground on which I would

appeal to the young men of St. Louis; namely, on the ground of their social importance as a class, and their individual influence as members of that class.

In other cities, the young man may plead his insignificance as an excuse for self-indulgence in those things which offer a bad example to others. He may say that the institutions of society are so fixed, that nothing he can do will affect them; that the interests of society are in the hands of older persons and must be protected by them. But here it is not so. Our institutions are not fixed; our standard of morality is not established, and it is chiefly for the young men of this city to say what it shall hereafter be. Whether they know it or not, they are doing a large part in giving direction to public opinion and establishing the standard of public morality. Taken together, they are the strength of the city; individually, every one of them has a part to perform.

You may think that this is an exaggerated statement; but it is not. The character of our young men is now, and for a long time to come must be, the character of our city. They must settle the point whether intemperance, dissipation, licentiousness, profanity, gambling, and the like, shall be the order of the day, or, instead of them, religion, good order, sobriety, chastity, and other virtues which belong to the gentleman and Christian. It is for them to determine what shall be the standard of refinement and education among us; whether we shall be a mere money-loving community, buying and selling to get gain, or a community in which it is necessary for a man to be educated in order to be respected, to be refined in order to be tolerated. It is for them to say whether literature and the fine arts, learning and science, shall take firm root among us, or struggle for a feeble existence as they do now. Do you say that such things properly devolve upon the older and wealthier members of the community? We answer, that, for several years past, those of our older citizens who have large wealth at their command, have been giving evidence of their interest in the welfare of our city. Some of them have shown great liberality towards our infant institutions of learning and benevolence, and those who have not yet done so are probably only waiting for some opportunity of enlarged action. We beg them not to wait until the hour of death. It is far better to give than to bequeathe; better, both as a service of God and as a benefit to mankind We would also remind you, that among the wealthier there are found many who yet belong to the ranks of young men, or who are just passing into middle life. It is to them that we look, and not in vain, to become leaders in every good movement, promoters of every good cause. That they will respond to the call, we have every reason to believe. The wealth which they are rapidly accumulating in our thriving city, they will generously use for the city's best advancement. They are already doing so, and we trust that it will abound more and more. To what nobler use can they devote their growing fortunes, than to the furtherance of sound knowledge and useful information, in the city where they live. Their prosperity will deserve respect, their devotion to business will become a Christian calling, if, as they advance in the road to wealth, they plant the trees of knowledge and of virtue by the way-side for the benefit of those to come after them. We appeal to them, as being at the same time the young men and the influential men of our city. Let them deal towards this community with a liberal hand and a large heart, and they will find therein an exceeding great reward. They will find it in well-deserved respect; in the feeling that they labor, not for money, but for humanity; in the consciousness that by their prosperity society is blessed. I know that I speak to many such, and that my words do not fall upon unwilling ears. We have reason to hope that what they have done in time past is but the earnest of greater works in the time to come.

But neither from the older nor the wealthier classes can the chief influence come. It must chiefly proceed from that more numerous class, who are, comparatively speaking, beginners in life; who have but little to work with, except character and example; who must do their part towards forming the community aright, by forming themselves aright; who must elevate the general taste, by elevating their own taste; who must promote good morals, by making their own lives correct; who must advance education, by educating themselves; who must give a right direction, by themselves going in the right direction.

This is the great thing to be done, and this is what every one can do. Do you ask how? We answer, let every young man consider the great problem of life seriously and with care. Let him have a fixed aim; a purpose which he will accomplish, a work which he will do. Not the plan for a year only; not the purpose which to-morrow will change; but a fixed aim, a life-purpose, to which every thing shall be made to bend, which every thing shall be made to subserve. We need not say a good aim, a good purpose. I defy you to have any other, if you adopt it deliberately. You cannot make up your mind to the devotion of your lives to any mean or worthless pursuit, even if you try. You may do the thing itself; you may devote yourselves to mere labor, like a beast of burden; or to mere pleasure, like the worldling; or to iniquity, as though you loved it for its own sake. But this will not be from a fixed purpose, as your selected plan of life. It will be because you have no plan, because you are putting off to some more convenient season the claims of duty and religion. Bring yourselves to say, "This shall be my aim in life; this is the whole work which my whole life shall accomplish"; and as surely as your soul was made in the image of your God, you will turn your face heavenward. The great delusion of sin is this: we persuade ourselves that for a few months or years we may live without a fixed aim, and yet go in no fixed direction; that we may continue in certain wrong courses, indulging ourselves in sinful pleasures, giving ourselves only to worldly pursuits, and that by and by we will begin a new course with a higher aim in life. And so we go onward to our ruin. For he who has no fixed aim in a right direction may be sure that he is steadily going in a wrong. The strong folds of habit will gather round him; his moral tastes will be perverted; his influence will be exerted on the side of evil; his whole life will become a failure.

Throw your minds forward now, if you can, and in imagination place yourselves at the closing term of a long life. Let the three-score years pass over you, with all their varied cares and occupations, until the physical frame is already bowing under their influence, and the freshness of life has gone, and the account must, in the course of nature, soon be rendered in. Sit down as at that advanced age, in your counting-room, in your office, or at your own fireside, and let the former years pass in review before you, that you may read the record they are bearing onward to eternity. Let memory play a faithful part, until the whole picture of your life is held up before your mind's eye.

At first it comes indistinctly and in confused lines, but gradually more and more plain, until each object is distinctly seen, and each event distinctly remembered. The history of your life is before you, and, either for good or for evil, you are compelled to read it.

With what different feelings will it be, according to the manner in which your lives have been spent! If it is the history of a childhood full of promise, in which fond parents expended the treasures of love upon you, and in which the early development of your minds gave earnest of a vigorous and manly character, but from which you passed to the years of wayward and undisciplined youth; if, as the history goes on, it tells you of one who advanced in years, but not in knowledge, — who was industrious because he was compelled to be, to gain a living, and whose surplus means, large or small, were expended for idle and unprofitable pleasures, or for foolish and sinful indulgences; if it tells of one who had no fixed plan of life, but went forward as he was carried by the force of example, to which he submitted himself, even when he despised it; if it tells you of one whose place in the world was merely to do a certain amount of daily work and to be paid for it, but whose influence upon the real interests of society was either negative or baneful; if it tells you of a man whose name is not written with honor upon any public record, or upon any enterprise of usefulness or philanthropy; if, as you read the continued history, you see that, so far as all the great interests of man are concerned, — education, refinement, art, morality, religion, — the man of whom you are reading might as well never have lived at all, — that in all these respects his history is a blank, — that for all the real uses of life his existence has been a failure and a mistake; — young man! if this history should be the record of your own life, with what feelings would you read it? Was it for no more than this that you were placed here? Are you satisfied to think of so tame and insignificant a result of a life which begins with so many aspiring hopes? Is this to be the end of all your youthful ambition, — a record stale, flat, and unprofitable, which you yourself are ashamed to read, and which no one else will either read or remember?

Yet I have spoken of no crime. The record which we have now been reading is not so much of a wicked life, as of one passed in the common routine of events, with nothing either very good or very bad to mark it. To him who is passing such a life, it seems well enough. The finger of scorn is not pointed at him; he holds a position comparatively respectable; he earns his own living, occasionally helps a friend or neighbor, and never does any thing to bring absolute disgrace upon his name. There are so many whose lives are worse, that he is tolerably well satisfied with himself. But how meagre and unsatisfactory must the whole appear, when it passes under that stern review at the last! When the close of life comes, can any one of us be satisfied with its result, unless we feel that in some respect it has been a good thing for the cause of humanity and for the glory of God, that we have lived?

What, then, must be the feelings of him,

who reads the records of a life, not only worthless, but wicked? if that too faithful memory recalls days of folly and nights of crime? if dissipation, and revelry, and licentiousness, and blasphemy, and violation of trust, and broken promises, are the headings of the chapters, as he reads from page to page? Think of one who, in the silent loneliness of old age, broods over recollections such as these! He feels that he does not comprehend the depth to which he has fallen; the light of eternity is needed to reveal that to him; but he knows enough to be covered with shame, and the despondency of his heart is but little better than despair. Young man! kneel down and pray to your God, that he may save you from such a close of life as this! Pray for early death, for poverty, for suffering, for ignominy, rather than to be left in the darkness of that sorrow. For nothing can come to you in this world, which would not seem joy and happiness in comparison with this.

And what difference will it make, if such a review of sin comes before you in the gilded hall of wealth, or under the destitution of poverty? Will the gold adorn the record itself, so that you can read it pleasantly? Will it become an illuminated page, because the headings of those fearful chapters are embellished with bright coloring, and the volume encased in costly binding? Will "innocence seduced," and "virtue corrupted," and "religion profaned," appear less hateful on that account? Or will they not seem rather to be written in burning letters; illuminated indeed, but as if by the fierceness of fire? You may bribe the world, and buy its good opinion, but can you bribe your conscience? Can you circumvent your God?

Turn away from so sad a picture. Let the retrospect of our life come under what circumstances it may, in riches or in poverty, in a position of great influence, or in one of comparative obscurity; but let it be the retrospect of a life well spent, — a life of truth, of honor and sobriety, — a life of manly earnestness to do whatever we were able to remove the sufferings of humanity, to educate ourselves in practical goodness, to promote the cause of morality and religion. It may recall no great deeds of philanthropy, but if the chambers of our imagination contain no pictures of guilt,—if in the last review of life we are able honestly to say, "Religion and morality have not suffered at our hands, but by a daily good example, and by the faithful use of whatever means and influence we possessed, we have done whatever we could for God and for Christ's sake,"—then will the closing days of life be to us as the beginning of heaven; and when the world begins to recede from our eyes, our hearts will be filled with the peace which passeth all understanding.

I speak unto you, therefore, young men, that ye *may become* strong; that the word of God may abide in you, and that ye may overcome the wicked one. Love not the world, neither the things that are in the world. For all that is in the world, the lust of the flesh, and the lust of the eyes, and the pride of life, is not of the Father, but is of the world. And the world passeth away, and the lust thereof, but he that doeth the will of God abideth for ever.

LECTURE II.

SELF-EDUCATION.

"Get wisdom; get understanding. . . . . . Take fast hold of instruction; let her not go; keep her, for she is thy life."—Prov. iv. 5, 13.

My subject for this evening is self-education. The word is often applied to the acquisition of knowledge alone, but we now give it a more extended and more important application. Not only the intellect needs to be educated, but also the tastes, the affections, the manners, and the character. There is diversity of talents, of gifts, and of opportunities. It is our duty to use those which we have, to the best advantage, and thereby to secure their enlargement.

The majority of young men in this country are led, either by necessity or choice, to enter upon the active duties of life with an imperfect education, and comparatively unformed in character. In older countries a greater degree of development is required in advance; but in this new and vigorous land, it is enough if one is able to do the task which immediately devolves upon him. He is then set to work, and is very often kept so constantly employed, that it requires a good deal of resolution to find either time or inclination for any thing else. There is a strong temptation to give up the leisure time which comes, either to natural indolence or to frivolous amusement. If the temptation is yielded to, the result is constant deterioration of character; and, instead of educating himself, the young man is soon diverted from the best purposes of life, and brought under influences which forbid either his moral or intellectual elevation.

The great fault of the young under such circumstances, as we have already said, is the want of a fixed aim, and of resolution in keep ing it. There is a want also of self-reliance They too readily yield their own principles and purposes to those around them, and instead of forming themselves after the model which they held before them at first, they suffer themselves to be formed by others. It is here that the importance of self-education is seen.

The young should begin with a standard of excellence before them, to which they should resolutely conform themselves. There should be a fixed determination to make the best of one's self, in whatever circumstances we are placed. Let the young man determine, that whatever he undertakes, he will do well; that he will make himself master of the business upon which he enters, and always prepare himself for advancement by becoming worthy of it. It is not opportunity of rising which is wanting, so often as the ability to rise. It is not the patronage of friends and the outward helps of fortune, to which the prominent men of our country owe their elevation, either in wealth or influence, so much as to their own vigorous and steady exertions. We hear a great many complaints, both among young men and old, of the favoritism of fortune and the partiality of the world; but my observation leads me to believe, that to a great extent those who deserve promotion obtain it. Those who are worthy of confidence will have confidence reposed in them. Those who give evidence of ability and industry will find opportunity enough for their exercise.

Take a familiar illustration. A young man engages in some business, who is in every respect a beginner in life. A common-school education is all that he can boast. He knows almost nothing of the world, and very little of the occupation on which he has entered. He performs his duty from day to day sufficiently well, and does what he is expected to do. But it does not enter his mind to do any thing beyond what is required, nor to enlarge his capacities by reading or reflection. He is, at the best, a steady, plodding man, who will go forward, if at all, very slowly, and will rise, if at all, to no great elevation. He is not the sort of person who is looked for to occupy a higher position. One opportunity of advancement after another may come directly in his reach, and he asks the influence of friends to push him upward. They give it feebly, because they have no great hope of success, and are not confident in their own recommendation. As a matter of course, some one else, more competent or more earnest, steps in before him, and then we hear renewed complaints of favoritism and injustice. Such an one may say in his defence, that he has been guilty of no dereliction of duty; that no fault has been found with him, and that therefore he was entitled to advancement. But this does not follow. Something more than that may reasonably be required. To bestow increased confidence, we require the capacity and habit of improvement in those whom we employ. The man who is entitled to rise, is one who is always enlarging his capacity, so that he is evidently able to do more than he is actually doing.

In every department of business, whether of the mechanic or merchant, or whatever it may be, there is a large field of useful knowledge, which should be carefully explored. An observing eye and an inquiring mind will always find enough for examination and study It may not seem to be of immediate use; it may have nothing to do with this week's or this year's duty; yet it is worth knowing. The mind gains vigor by the inquiry, and the hand itself obtains greater skilfulness by the intelligence which directs it.

The result is all the difference between a mere drudge and an intelligent workman; between the mere salesman or clerk, and the enterprising merchant; between the obscure and pettifogging lawyer, and the sagacious, influential counsellor. It is the difference between one who deserves to be, and will be, stationary in the world, and one who, having determined to make the best of himself, will continually rise in influence and true respectability. This whole difference we may see every day among those who have enjoyed nearly equal opportunities. We may allow something to what are called the accidents of social influence, and the turns of fortune. But after all fair allowance has been made, we shall find that the great cause of difference is in the men themselves. Let the young man who is beginning life put away from him all notions of advancement without desert. A man of honorable feelings will not even desire it. He will rather shrink from engaging in duties which he is not able fairly to perform. He will first of all secure to himself the capacity of performing them, and then he is ready for them whenever they come.

The truth of what I have now said will be admitted by most persons, with application to the business in which each one is engaged. It will be admitted that the young mechanic or the young merchant should inform himself, as soon and as thoroughly as possible, in the whole range of the occupation in which he has embarked. Every one can see the direct utility of this. But when a larger application is given to the same principles, it is often disputed. It is thought quite unnecessary for those who belong to the working world to trouble themselves about general information, or to educate themselves beyond their immediate walk in life. There is almost a prejudice against one who devotes much attention to subjects of art or science, or general literature, as though such occupations were inconsistent with the ordinary routine of business life.

Nor would I meet this prejudice by too positive denial. I am willing to allow that he who has his own way to make in the world, must fix his eye intently upon some one object of pursuit, and not suffer his mind to be distracted from it by any thing else. That must be his work in life, to which every other pursuit must for the time be subordinate. Particularly is this true to the beginner. His heart must be in his business. He must lay hold upon it with a grasp that nothing can loosen. He must attend to its smallest details, in preference to things which are in themselves a thousand times more important. For the present duty is always that which must be performed. We cannot excuse ourselves for its neglect because it is insignificant or disagreeable, nor because something else more pleasant and seemingly more profitable offers itself. Especially when we are employed by others, under an arrangement to do a specific work for which we receive compensation, we are bound to perform every part of it faithfully, although to our own loss and discomfort. We have no right even to improve ourselves at the expense of those whom we serve. Nor are we wise if we suffer ourselves to be diverted from the occupation which we have deliberately chosen, for the cultivation of taste or the acquisition of knowledge.

He who neglects his Coke upon Littleton for the beauties of Shakspeare may be commended for his taste, but will never do much as a lawyer. He who loves the books in his own library so much, that he turns over the books in his counting-room with disgust, may become a scholar, but not a merchant. Whatever is our occupation, therefore, particularly while we are young, should be made our chief work. It should stand first in our thoughts. We should never neglect it for the sake of any incidental advantages, however great they may appear. But in all this there is nothing inconsistent with the work of self-education. This steadfastness of purpose, this close adhe rence to a fixed plan of life, is in itself a good discipline, both for the mind and character.

Let us make our work a part of the general plan of duty and self-improvement, and we can bring under the same plan all other things which tend to the same result. There is no necessity of one part of our duty interfering with another. Rightly done, the proper performance of each part will help all the rest.

I know the objection which immediately arises, when any plan of self-education is proposed. It is the want of time. But, generally speaking, it would come nearer the truth to say "want of inclination." Very few persons are so burdened with work that they cannot find one or two hours in the day at their own command. It requires, indeed, some resolution to use such time according to a regular plan of self-education; but in that case we ought not to plead the want of time, but of purpose. The proper and judicious use of one hour a day is enough to make any of us well-educated men in the course of a few years. Make the trial faithfully, and you will be astonished how much can be accomplished in that one hour a day. Some of the profoundest scholars and most voluminous writers in the world, have confined themselves to their study but two or three hours daily. The rest of their time has been given to the active pursuits of life.

There is, undoubtedly, a part of the year in which young men cannot find the hour of which I now speak. There is a part of the year in which they are overworked as if they were beasts of burden. It is a pity, and it seems to me wrong that it is so. It is often a permanent injury to their health, and such seasons of overworking leave them in a state of body and mind most unfavorable for the work of self-improvement, when the time for it is again allowed. He who has been thus crowded and overladen for two or three months, is apt to feel, when the burden is thrown off, that he can relish nothing but frivolous amusements or complete idleness. Thus, a few months' excessive working becomes an excuse for wasting the leisure time of the whole year. But it needs no argument to show the folly of this. When every moment is occupied with work, we cannot be blamed for having no leisure. But when the work ceases and the leisure comes, it should be all the more diligently used. The great majority of young men in this city have their evenings to themselves, if nothing more, during seven or eight months of the year. Let one half of that time be spent with a view to self-education, in the acquisition of knowledge and in the improvement of the mind, and how great a revolution would be wrought by a few years in our city. What a noble class of young men would then come forward to occupy the prominent places in society. How quickly would all the interests of science, of literature, of art and philanthropy, flourish among us. The foolish and wicked dissipations of city life would rapidly decline, and the moral wilderness would blossom as the rose.

We do not deny the necessity of amusement and of recreation. Neither bodily nor mental health can be secured without them.

But if our recreations are judiciously selected, we shall find time enough for them, without interference with more important things.

It is when we make a business of pleasure that it becomes hurtful. It is when we seek for amusement in the haunts of dissipation, or with wicked companions, that it becomes sinful. A sensible man can find time enough and ways enough for all the recreation he needs, without encroachment upon the real work of life. I have, indeed, met with a few instances in which persons are kept so constantly at work that they have almost no time to themselves. I know young men who, through a greater part of the year, are so overtasked, that when the Sunday comes they have heart for nothing and are almost fit for nothing, except sleeping or idleness, and who decline coming to church because they cannot keep awake. In such cases their employers are guilty of great sin. But they are the exceptions which serve to show that it is very different with the majority. With nearly all there is time enough for the common work of the day and for needful recreation, and a surplus of one or two hours at least for self-improvement.

We again admit that the proper use of that hour or two requires a resolute purpose. It must often be done as a duty, rather than as a pleasure. But it may be done, and by those who take the right view of life it will be done. The end in view is worth striving for. It is to make ourselves intelligent, thoughtful, and well-educated men.

It is to raise ourselves above mere servants and laborers into a position of influence and growing usefulness. It is to make men of ourselves, and to fit us for the duties which men alone can do. If I could induce all who hear me to spend the evenings of this coming winter with a direct view to self-education, they would have reason to thank me for it all the rest of their lives. The result of the whole life would be thereby changed, for this is a work which, once entered upon, will not be abandoned.

He who begins to grow in knowledge and

refinement will continue to advance, because he learns to love the pursuit. I ask you, therefore, to think carefully upon this subject. Do you not need this self-education?

Are you satisfied to remain as you now are?

Can you not see that your usefulness, your happiness, and your real respectability would be indefinitely increased, by devoting a part of each day to the acquisition of knowledge and the improvement of your mind?

None can be so blind as not to see this; a great many are too indolent to act accordingly.

But, first of all, as the beginning and foundation of all improvement, is the distinct acknowledgment of its necessity. To acknowledge it in general terms, is not enough. It must be felt. As we feel the necessity of food when we are hungry, so must we feel the necessity of improvement, before we shall succeed in gaining it. The young are prevented from feeling it, chiefly by two causes; sometimes by self-conceit; sometimes by having too low a standard of excellence before them. We are apt to think better of ourselves in early life than at any subsequent period. As we grow older and wiser we feel our deficiencies more, for it requires a certain degree of knowledge to know how much is to be learned. Our ideal of excellence also remains low until the mind and character are developed. Thus, from the two causes together, we are easily satisfied in youth with attainments of which in after years we would feel ashamed. This same experience we go through, most probably, whether we are scholars, or men of business, or men of the world. Accordingly you will find many young men, who account themselves complete merchants and accomplished gentlemen, when in fact they are but beginners, and perhaps give but a bad promise for the future in either department.

It requires a great deal to make an accomplished gentleman. It is not only to wear good clothing in a way which shows that one is used to it, or to be free from awkwardness in manners, although this is something. There must be an accomplished mind. There must be delicacy of feeling and refinement of taste. For all this will show itself in the manners of a gentleman. Without it there may be a kind of polish, — that which the dancing-master and the clothing-store can give, — which is the highest ambition of many persons to attain. Many a dapper and spruce young gentleman is as proud of its attainment, as if it were a sufficient passport to perfect gentility; but it is not so. To be an accomplished gentleman, one must be a thinking and well-educated man. No external polish can take the place of the thoughtful mind which gives a manly expression to the features, and the refinement of taste which bestows grace and gentleness upon the deportment.

In like manner does it require a great deal to make a complete merchant. Merely to buy and to sell, to know how to make a shrewd bargain, to understand the quality of the common articles of merchandise, is very far from being all. All of this may be learned by one who cannot speak his own language correctly, and who has no conception of the real uses of trade. Commerce is the great civilizing agent of the world. Let it work as it ought to do, hand in hand with knowledge and virtue and religion, and it is the messenger of peace and good-will among men. The merchant who understands the nobleness of his calling, occupies a position far above that of mere buying and selling. He cannot be narrow-minded; he cannot stoop to the mean and tricky contrivances, by which men overreach each other. He is not contented merely to make money and to spend it. He takes a large view of society and its interests. His intercourse with different parts of the world frees his mind from prejudice, and prepares him to receive light from whatever quarter it may come. He feels it to be his duty to introduce into the community where he lives, all the means of improvement which are found elsewhere. Thus regarded, commerce becomes an nterchange of ideas as well as of goods. But to make it so, those who conduct it must be men of intelligence, of refinement, and of truth. The young man who enters upon such a career should feel respect for his calling. He should determine to qualify himself by self-culture, by the acquisition of knowledge and the practice of virtue, to become a complete merchant, to rise to the head of his profession. No man need to have a more honorable ambition than that. It will task all his powers; it will give room for the exercise of his best faculties and for the use of his highest attainments. How sad it is to see so many, with such a career before them, contented to remain all their lives with no higher ideas than to write a good hand, or to make a close bargain! There is no scholarly profession better calculated to enlarge the mind and elevate the character than the pursuits of commerce; yet they are often debased to the most pitiful uses, and those who engage in them often remain through their whole lives ignorant and uneducated.

To prevent such a result the young man who enters upon this career should take himself in hand. He should place his standard of excellence very high, and use all the means in his reach to attain it. Chiefly through self-culture, in the daily acquisition of knowledge, and by a manly and honorable course of life, he should make himself worthy of his calling, and of the highest honors it can bring. How different will be the whole tenor of his life, if he enters upon it with such views as these! How easy will it be to resist the enticements of pleasure and the allurements of vice! With what instinctive disgust will he shrink from low associates and the vulgarity of dissipation. With such an end in view, how easy will it be to find time for reading and opportunity for self-improvement.

With such a purpose in his heart from day to day, he is secured from the temptations to which youth is chiefly exposed, and has only to press forward to secure the highest reward which a true ambition can ask.

We might go through nearly the same ourse of remark with regard to the mechanic. The mere workman does not seem to occupy an elevated place in society; although, if he does his work well and conducts himself with honesty and sobriety, he occupies a place of usefulness and is worthy of respect. By the force of character, if he has no other advantages, he may work his way to confidence and to high estimation among men. But there is no necessity of his remaining a mere workman. In this country, as large and as good a field of action is open before him as before any other. If he has the natural ability and will use the opportunities of improvement offered to him, he may rise to as great height as he can reasonably desire. Look at the triumphs of art and the perfection to which the science of mechanics has been brought in our day. Look at the names which society delights to honor, in this country and in England, and see how many are of men who began at the work-bench or at the forge, and who, by the application of their minds to the work in which they engaged, carved for themselves a way to distinction and usefulness. The name of "mechanic" has long ceased to be one of social contempt. Let the young mechanic learn to be a thinking and observing man, and he will find as easy and as rapid progress in the world as through any other calling. There is certainly nothing in work itself to degrade the mind; but, on the contrary, we are more apt to find the development of practical and sound udgment in the workshop than in the study. Only let the same pains be taken to improve the mind, and the workingman would have the advantage. We admit, as we have already done, that it requires strong resolution in one who has been closely employed all day, to turn his attention to the work of self-culture at night. But it is certainly not impossible nor impracticable, for many do it; and my object in speaking is to inspire such resolution in those who hear me. If it were a thing that could be done without effort, it would probably be not so well worth the doing.

There never was a country or an age, in which greater opportunities were offered to young men than our own. The age is one in which all the elements of advancing civilization are at work. Our country is, perhaps, the only one in the world which offers a fair and equal field for the competition of all who enter upon it. There is every excitement for the young man to lay hold upon his work in life, with the vigorous determination to make the most of himself and to play his part in the world manfully. Society places no obstacles in the way of his advancement. There are no serious difficulties to be overcome, except in himself. If he remains obscure and useless, it is his own fault. If he fails to become a well-educated and influential man, it is not for the want of opportunity, but of industry and enterprise.

Look particularly at the position which our own city occupies, and see if a young man could reasonably ask a nobler sphere of action, or better opportunities of self-advancement, than are offered here. In this great Western valley, which is destined to become the garden of the world, and will contain in itself a greater population than that of the whole United States at this time, our city is one of the chief points of influence. By a remarkable growth it now contains nearly a hundred thousand inhabitants, and every thing indicates that its future increase will be as rapid as the past. We shall have no reason to be surprised if in a few years its present number is doubled. A grand system of internal improvement is now begun, by which, if we take hold of it as we ought, this city will become the centre of a commerce as great as that of our largest Eastern cities now. In ten years' time its railroads will stretch from the sources to the mouth of the Mississippi, and from the Atlantic to the Pacific Ocean. The imagination loses itself in the grandeur of such enterprises; but they seem chimerical only because they are so great. They are perfectly practicable, for the resources at command are equal to the work, and the benefits realized at each advancing step will secure their ultimate completion.

A prudent man may hesitate to say what the West and its leading cities will become, for fear of being accounted visionary. But I doubt if any expectations have been formed so sanguine that they will not be accomplished and surpassed.

But with the possibility of such a future

before us, what manner of men ought those to be to whom the vital interests of society are intrusted? In what manner shall they do their part now, so as to secure the prosperity for which we hope, and prepare themselves to meet its responsibilities? What kind of young men are needed in an infant city which promises to grow to such a robust manhood? It is not those who spend their time in the tavern and at the billiard-table; not those whose best ambition is to make a good figure in the ball-room and the dance; not those who pride themselves in their dress and equipage; not those whose only ambition in life is to become rich; but we need those who, keeping themselves free from idle dissipation, begin their career with frugality and honorable industry, and, in every step of their progress, take pains to educate themselves, to develop their minds, to mature their character, to strengthen their judgment; so that, as their duties in life become more important, they will be able to perform them with faithfulness. We need young men who have an honorable ambition in life; determined to be useful according to their ability, and to increase their ability by diligent self-culture and the practice of virtue. Give us a class of young men such as this, and what a glorious future ours would be. For I would again say, it is upon the young men that it chiefly depends. The older and wealthier portion of the community may do their part; but the tone of society, the intellectual and moral character of our city, ten or twenty years hence, depends chiefly upon those who are young now. Almost every thing that is needed for the moral and intellectual growth of this community is yet to be done. A beginning is scarcely made. Institutions of almost every kind are yet to be founded, or, if already begun, need to be fostered and strengthened. In every department of philanthropy, of religious and moral enterprise, laborers are needed. But still more than this. There is need of a more elevated public opinion, of greater refinement of taste, of a higher standard of morality, of more profound respect for religion. We need an army drawn out in battle array against the six hundred bar-rooms of the city, and against the thousand demoralizing influences so busily at work among us. Where shall we find the growing strength that is needed against the growing evil, except in the vigor of youthful manliness? Where shall we find recruits for that peaceful army, except among young men, whose own interests are chiefly in peril?

Finally, let us remember that the chief influence which every one of us exerts is the influence of character. This is an individual work, and it is the most important work that any one of us can do. We do it faithfully, in proportion as we keep ourselves from the pursuit of folly, from the commission of sin; in proportion as we grow in excellence and usefulness; in proportion to our attainment of the Christian graces and to our practice of the Christian virtues. Young men, what motive is wanting to secure your diligence and faithfulness, when the very same course of life will conduct you to self-respect, to honor among men, and to the approbation of God? Therefore, get wisdom, get understanding. Take fast hold of instruction; let her not go; keep her, for she is thy life.

LECTURE III.

LEISURE TIME.

"See then that ye walk circumspectly, not as fools, but as wise, redeeming the time." — Eph. v. 15, 16.

The great difference between young men, with regard to the work of self-improvement, comes from the different manner in which they employ their leisure time. The working day is very much the same to all. A specific task is to be done, and the motive for its faithful performance is so urgent, that it is not likely to be neglected, except by those who have already taken a good many steps towards becoming worthless. But in the manner of spending their leisure time, the greatest possible difference is found, and from this, in the course of years, proceeds almost the whole difference among men. He who spends his leisure time well, is an improving man; he who spends it badly, is one who will remain stationary or go downward.

By leisure time, we mean, chiefly, the evening and the Sabbath. For although, during the day, there are a great many hours quite idle, the etiquette of business is understood to forbid the young man to do any thing with such unemployed time, except to lounge about the store or stand upon the pavement. I am not able to perceive the necessity of this; but as the rule is universal, I take for granted that it is founded on right. Otherwise, I should suppose that it would be far better both for employers and employed, when perhaps five or six young men have almost nothing to do, for several months in the year, that they should be encouraged in some regular plan of self-improvement; but having no practical knowledge upon the subject, I do not venture to express an opinion.

The leisure time of which we speak at present, is that which young men have entirely at their own control. It does not belong to the business hours, and they may use it to good or bad purpose or to no purpose, just as they please. From the manner in which they please to use it, I repeat, the ultimate difference in their characters and their prospects in life will chiefly depend.

This may not at first be admitted. Young men are apt to think that, if their working hours are well employed, it is no matter what becomes of the rest; that it is their own time, for which they are responsible to nobody. But they will discover, before life closes, that they are responsible for it to their own consciences and to God. The sum of their responsibility and the result of their whole lives, for good or evil, depends upon this more than upon any thing else.

We grant that a single evening, whether idled away or well used, is no very great matter; yet perhaps that single evening may bring the commencement of a long train of vices, which ends in complete ruin. We grant that a single Sunday, devoted to amusement, may have no great influence upon the general character; yet that one day misspent may be the first step towards a life of irreligion. But it is not of single violations of duty that we are now speaking, nor of the manner in which we spend the leisure time of a single day. I speak of the habit of life. How are your evenings generally spent? To what employment is your Sunday generally devoted? Answer that question for a year, and I will tell you, with almost absolute certainty, whether you are growing better or worse in character; whether the tendency of your whole lives is upward or downward. Answer that question for a series of ten years, and we need nothing else to determine the degree of your real respectability and usefulness in the world. If I am to decide upon a man's character, I desire to know nothing more than this, — How are his evenings and his Sundays passed?

It is for the want of paying regard to this, that we are so often deceived in the real character of business men. We see one, for instance, who is every day punctually at his work, and who, through all the business hours, is found in his proper place. He is attentive and industrious there, and we pronounce him a good business man and repose unlimited confidence in him. All at once, we find that his character is rotten at the core. He abuses our confidence, neglects our interests, and proves altogether unworthy of trust. We are completely astonished at such a development. We speak of it as if it were a sudden change of character, for which it is impossible to account. But if we had known, for several years before, to what pursuits his leisure time was devoted, we should have anticipated the result, long before it actually came. There probably has been for many years some corrupting influence, some vile habit of dissipation or self-indulgence, by which the character has been gradually undermined; and although the fall itself seems to be sudden, the causes which led to it have long been at work. Our knowledge of the world should teach us never to put great confidence in any man's virtue or honesty, unless we know to what pursuits his leisure time is given. Then it is that his real tendencies show themselves. Then it is, when no longer under the external pressure of business, that he acts himself out most freely; and if you find that his tastes are then depraved, that his pleasures are low, that his companions are dissipated or vulgar, you may mark him as an unsafe man, who, sooner or later, will prove himself unworthy of respect or confidence.

Take, for illustration, two general plans of life in the employment of leisure time. We need not select extreme cases, either of good or bad, but such as are met with in every day's observation.

There are many who, when the day's work is over, are guided by no particular rule with regard to their evenings. They have no feeling of duty upon the subject. To get rid of the time in some way, so that it may not be tedious, is their only thought. A half-hour or more they idle about their hotels in very unprofitable conversation and in laughter, which is apt to be loud in proportion as the cause which excites it is objectionable. Thence they stroll in groups of two or three together, perhaps to some stylish saloon, either with or without the intention of drinking, but generally it results in their "taking something," and with some other groups, engaged in the same employment of killing time, the conversation becomes still more unprofitable and the mirth more boisterous. The billiard-room or bowling-alley demands their next attention, and there, perhaps, the rest of the evening is spent; or if not, the transition is to some other amusements of about the same grade. Occasionally a little improvement is made upon this, by giving the evening and a great part of the night to the ball-room, where there is at least the refining influence of ladies' society, and, generally speaking, the absence of vulgarity and dissipation. Occasionally the concert-room affords a more refined and unobjectionable employment, or the theatre mingles with the entertainment some elements of instruction and intellectual enjoyment. Occasionally, when these different resorts become tiresome or too expensive, or when some particular temptation comes in the way, the evening is given to what is called a frolic, in which the elements of sin are mingled far enough to give piquancy and novelty to the entertainment, without awakening the severe reproaches of conscience.

Such is the history of the evening. We have not spoken of intemperance, of gambling and licentiousness, for these do not come till afterwards. We are speaking only of that mode of life into which young men fall, because they have no particular rule of conduct, no fixed principle of life. Their Sundays will be in general of the same sort, with perhaps a greater touch of respectability, resulting from their early associations with the day. They rise very late; spend an unusual time over the newspaper; devote three or four hours to novel-reading, and two or three more, perhaps, after the dinner hour has been prolonged as much as possible, to an afternoon ride, in the progress of which it will be strange if something very much like dissipation does not occur. Sometimes, but probably at long intervals, they find leisure to visit a church; but they do not feel quite comfortable there: for if the minister is faithful, he touches their consciences too much, and if not faithful, he is sure to be dull; so that their visits become less and less frequent, until they completely cease. Sometimes they find their way to their counting-rooms or other places of business, and either by themselves, or with some customer, who has been introduced at a side door, they devote a few hours to their ordinary week-day work. Sometimes, and more frequently as time progresses, they join regular pleasure-parties, which, upon the steamboat or elsewhere, are contrived for the profanation of the Sabbath upon a large scale.

We have not here spoken of an extreme case, although tolerably bad. You will find a great many such, among those who call themselves respectable and moral young men You will also find a great many who are no longer young, but whose children are growing up around them, the history of whose Sundays and other leisure time is very much what has now been given.

The question we have now to ask is, What must be the effect of such a manner of life upon the whole character? Take a series of years, and what must be its influence upon the mind and heart? Is a man likely to grow better under this discipline, or rather this want of discipline, or is he not quite certain to grow worse? Is he in a course of self-education which will result in manliness of character, refinement of taste, true elegance of manners, or largeness of thought? Is he likely to retain his self-respect, his purity of feeling, or his scrupulousness of conscience? Is he on the road to become a useful and good man, or the contrary? I think that the questions scarcely need an answer. They answer themselves, or if not, you have only to look upon those who try the experiment, and you will find an answer to fill you with sadness and regret.

Take, then, an illustration of a different course, and, again, take not an extreme case, such as might never occur in real life, but such as may be met with every day. It would be easy to describe a manner of life entirely free from all follies, in which not a day nor an hour is wasted; in which the whole energies are devoted to usefulness and self-improvement. But a model character like this is so rarely met with, that it seems like an imaginary picture, and its perfection causes a feeling of discouragement. As a teacher of morality, I would not be unreasonable in exaction. It is not well to expect too much. Something may be allowed to waywardness and youthful irresolution, and to the natural love of amusement.

It is well, however, sometimes to hold before us an ideal of unsullied excellence, of unstained purity, of undivided allegiance to duty. It would be well for us to picture to ourselves what a young man might become, if his whole heart were given to the pursuit of goodness and wisdom. If we could follow such a one, as he resists one temptation after another, as he adds to his daily store of useful knowledge, as he cultivates in himself every Christian grace and manly virtue, conforming himself diligently to that standard of life which the Gospel has ordained, it would be impossible not to feel respect for the heroism of his daily life, and admiration for the victory which he daily obtains. Such a contemplation would be a rebuke to our own indifference, and would make us feel how far short we are falling of our duty. We wonder that there are not more who take hold of life with this spirit. We wonder that there are so few who determine to make the very best of themselves, to make the most of their intellectual and moral strength in the service of God and man. But it is not one in a thousand, — no, nor in ten thousand, — who can honestly say that he is doing so. We excuse ourselves in so many deliberate omissions of duty, we waste so much time for the want of system in spending it, we allow so many faults of character for the want of resolution in correcting them, that, even when our general intention is good, we do not rise to one half the excellence of which we are capable.

In our present treatment of the subject, however, while we would make things better if we could, let us take them as they are. We do not figure to ourselves, therefore, a model young man, in whom there are no faults and who never wastes an hour of his time; but one who is guided by prudence and a sense of duty in his ordinary life; who takes pains to avoid the follies and dissipations which undermine the character, and to educate himself as a man and as a Christian, by the attainment of useful information. After his day's work is done, we may leave him sufficient time for rest and recreation. We do not limit him too closely, as to the number of hours in the week to be allowed for such purposes; only let him remember one thing, to carry his conscience with him wherever he goes and to whatever amusement he enters upon; for conscience belongs to our leisure not less than to our working time. He keeps himself away, therefore, from every haunt of vice. He avoids bad companions and takes pains to select good society. If some of his time is spent idly, no part of it will be spent badly; and after all allowance of this sort has been made, he will find a part of every day and a great many hours in every week, for judicious reading and study. The general purpose of self-education is never forgotten, and more or less rapidly the work is accomplished. His Sundays are spent either in good society of friends and kindred, or in the perusal of books, chosen with a view to instruction rather than amusement; or in the performance of some work of Christian charity and kindness. His church will not be neglected, but, as a regular habit, either once or twice in the Sunday he goes there, not only as a habit, but for the worship of God and to seek his blessing.

Surely we have described no standard of ideal excellence here. Many would say that it is but a tame and insufficient character, which the pulpit ought not to hold up for imitation. It is the least that might be expected of one educated by Christian parents, and who acknowledges his responsibility to God. Yet, imperfect as it is, it is far above the actual attainments of the majority of young men, and a wonderful improvement in society would take place if they could be elevated even to this point.

But the more important remark to be made at present is this: That the result of such a course of life, followed through a series of eight or ten years, would be to elevate those who follow it in their own self-respect and in the respect of the community. They would, from year to year, become more intelligent, more thoughtful and better men. They would be removed further and further from the influences of vice; and would appear more and more as the friends of virtue.

Compare them, at the end of ten years, with that class of young men whom we described a few minutes ago. In the beginning of their career a careless observer would not have seen the difference in the direction they were taking. But the two roads which lie almost together at first, rapidly diverge from each other, until it appears that one of them has led to worthlessness and infamy, and the other to usefulness and virtue.

And wherein has the difference consisted? Simply in the different use of leisure time, in the different manner in which the evening and the Sunday have been passed. It is the difference between two or three hours a day well spent and the same time wasted. The whole problem of life has been settled by those few hours, which are generally thought of no importance, and which young men are apt to feel may be thrown away whenever they please.

The most obvious, and perhaps the most important means of self-improvement, is *reading*. Books are food to the mind. Well-selected books, like wholesome food, impart strength and vigor, and bring the mind to its full growth. But as all food is not wholesome, and we may use that which is poisonous or hurtful, so there is a great deal of reading which is poisonous and hurtful to the mind.

We would not condemn all fictitious works as belonging to this class. The taste for such writings, whether in prose or poetry, is as natural to us as any other intellectual tendency.

Particularly wnen we are young, they are received with a relish that no other books can impart. A great deal of the instruction that we receive comes in this form; and although we may admit that this mode of making study attractive and learning easy has been carried much too far, we should be quite unwise to reject it altogether.

I cannot help saying, however, although it is only by the way, that the inordinate love of novel-reading which marks this generation probably proceeds from the multiplication of juvenile books of fiction, of which our Sunday schools and day schools are full. One would think, to look at them, that there is no way of inculcating a good moral, except by clothing it in a fictitious tale of love and danger. Books of instruction are scarcely put into the hands of the young, unless they are first disguised. Then, like the sugar-covered medicine, they are taken; but unfortunately, by a perverse mental digestion, the medicinal properties are too often rejected and the sugar alone retained. Even arithmetic and geography are made to undergo a diluting and disguising process, so as to save the young, as far as possible, from all exertion of thought. It is not surprising that children educated in this way refuse to read, as they grow older, except under the same condition of being amused These remarks, however, are leading me away from my present subject.

We do not condemn the reading of fiction, as being in itself wrong or hurtful. Many books which come under this class may be read, not only with safety, but with profit, by almost any one. The danger arises in such reading, first, from its engrossing too much of our time, and secondly, from a bad selection of the books read.

No one need expect to become a wise or well-educated man by novel-reading. As giving rest or recreation to the mind it is very well, but not for substance of thought and maturity of intellect.

One might as well expect to gain strength to his body from sweetmeats and confectionery, as for his mind from works of fiction.

The very best of them should be used as an occasional refreshment; considered as the daily food, they are absolutely pernicious. The young person who becomes a confirmed novel-reader, with a work of fiction always on hand, undergoes a process of mental deterioration more rapidly than he is aware. You might as well expect to make a person religious, by the pitiful dilutions of Christianity which appear under the head of religious novels at the present day, as to educate yourselves by historical romances, — from Waverley down to the latest of the fruitful brain of James. He who is seeking for self-improvement will read them sparingly.

So much may be said even of the better class of fiction. But what shall we say of that, whose very touch is defilement? which we compliment if we only call it trash, and with which to become acquainted is to bid farewell to all purity of thought and all refinement of feeling? It would be better not to know how to read, than to read it. He who holds it in his hand is proclaiming his own vulgarity of taste, and is doing openly that which he should be ashamed to do in secret. I do not fear to speak too strongly. I have not read, if it were all told, a hundred pages of such literature in my life; yet I feel that even in that a serious mistake was committed, and it would have been far better not to have seen it. As iron-rust upon the hand, which stays there until it wears off, so is an impure thought suggested to the mind, or a vile picture painted upon the imagination. We would implore the young to keep their hands off from such books, and to turn their minds away from the pollution which such books bring. If you have already learned to enjoy reading them, you have reason to tremble for your safety. For he who relishes the record of that which is vile, is almost prepared, himself, to be guilty of the same vileness.

To form a more correct taste in reading is by no means difficult. At first it may require some effort, but, like every other habit, soon becomes easy and pleasant. Biography, history, the higher departments of polite literature, works of art and science, are within every one's reach. At first they may seem less attractive than the light and flashy reading, for which they are so much neglected; but in a little while they become far more interesting, and with every page you read, you feel that you are taking a step in knowledge and refinement. They may not come under the head of amusement, and it is not as such that I would recommend them, but experience will prove to you that they supply healthy recreation to the mind and prepare it for the returning duties of the next day, far better than books which produce an unhealthy excitement, or pleasures by which the body has been fatigued and the mind exhausted. It is not as amusement that we recommend them, but as a study, and as a means of self-education. Time enough for amusement may be found beside. Can we not spare one or two hours a day, if not as a pleasure, then as a duty, in preparing ourselves for the real work of life, for doing our part as men and as Christians in society. In an age like this, where knowledge is almost in the atmosphere we breathe, can we content ourselves with ignorance? In a country where a good education is an essential requisite to respectability and in which vulgar-minded and uninformed men find it every day harder to rise, shall we refuse to make the needful exertion to educate ourselves, so as to deserve respect and to command influence? If I am speaking to those who are indifferent to such things, my words will be in vain; but if you desire them, if you wish to deserve respect, if you wish to obtain influence, if you wish to become useful by the best exertion of your faculties, then you will be ready to take some pains in its accomplishment. You will not expect so great a result without systematic and long-continued effort.

Let me therefore advise you, as your friend, to use a part of every day for careful and studious reading. Begin, if you please, with one hour, or even with less, but let it be done as a duty. It will bring its enjoyment, but let it be done as a duty.

Let your first aim be to supply the deficiencies of early education. Do not smile at the suggestion of a grammar and dictionary. I know business men who cannot tell where the places with which they trade are situated, and who cannot write a commercial letter without violations both of good grammar and correct spelling. It would be no disgrace to them, I think, to have Murray and Webster within reach. To a shallow mind this may seem boy's work, but if you will read the lives of the most eminent scholars, you will find that they are always learners. The best educated man must frequently return to the rudiments of knowledge, to see that the foundation is well laid. How much more is such a course needful to those who have never gone beyond a common school education, and to whom even that was very imperfect.

Such is the case with the great majority of young men who enter upon business. They are not beyond the necessity of schooling. They need elementary instruction. They are uninformed upon subjects upon which continued ignorance is inexcusable. They are not to blame for this; but they are to blame if they take no pains to supply the acknowledged deficiency. There is no necessity for their remaining ignorant or uneducated. Nay, there is no excuse for it. The means of self-education are within reach of all, not only books, but teachers, if need be, and the only thing wanting is sufficient resolution and industry to use them.

As to the choice of books and the course of reading to be followed by each one, no general rule can be given. This must depend upon the taste and previous education of each individual. But every young man should have some method, both in the choice of books and in using them. Beside his lighter reading, which is partly for amusement's sake, let him always have some one book, at least, or some one branch of study, to which his careful attention is every day directed. He will reap from this a double benefit; first, in his direct improvement, in the discipline of his mind and in the acquisition of knowledge; and secondly, by the employment of time which might otherwise hang heavily upon his hands or be devoted to idle amusements, which lead to worse than idle results. He would also find himself, by such a course, removed from the worst temptations to which the young are exposed. Bad companionship in idle hours is the common way to ruin. But he who is daily elevating his mind, by reading and study, will soon lose the taste for such companionship. He will find no pleasure in vulgarity or dissipation, and no sympathy with those who are guilty of them. He will avoid the bar-room and gambling-table, as much through good taste as through good principle. He will therefore at the same time feel less temptation to do wrong and find greater enjoyment in doing right.

To secure this result, however, he must add to his daily reading one book, which by many is thought old-fashioned, but which is not yet, thank God, out of print. It is the cheapest book in the world, and from whatever point of view we regard it, the best. It is *the book*, the Bible. Considered as history, it is the oldest and best authenticated; considered as poetry, it is the noblest, the most original and exalted; considered as a system of morality, it is absolu:ely perfect; considered as religion, it is sufficient both for time and eternity.

Set aside, if you please, all thought of its divine authority, and regard it as you do other books, according to its intrinsic worth, and you will find that it deserves frequent perusal and careful study. Yet I fear that many persons have almost no acquaintance with it, except that which comes from the dim recollections of childhood. Its very sanctity repels them. But if they do not read it as the revelations of God and as a religious duty, it should be read for its own sake.

The book of Proverbs contains enough practical wisdom to carry any man successfully through the world. Seneca and Franklin cannot be read with one half the profit, even with regard to the conduct of this life alone. The young man who reads a chapter of it every day, will find that folly and sin become an uphill business. The book of Job is a key to the mysteries of Providence, as we see them all around us. The Prophecies, although obscure and difficult, fill the mind with pictures of heavenly glory and reveal to us the judgments of God.

But above all, the New Testament, to those who know how to prize simplicity of style and grandeur of thought, is an inexhaustible fund of instruction and delight. The character of Jesus Christ, if we could regard it simply as a historical fact, apart from its religious bearing, is worthy of never-ending study. It is the only perfect character ever delineated. If it were a fiction it would be wonderful; being true, it is miraculous. His words come to us, as a breathing from heaven. His life opens to us an acquaintance with heavenly existence.

Yet I believe, that, with the exception of those who have been led by religious experience to place their hopes of eternal life in the Gospel, there is no book which is estimated so far below its real and intrinsic merits as the Bible. I commend it to your reading, if not as a religious duty, as a means of self-education, for the refinement of your taste and for the general elevation of your character.

But consider it as a religious duty, and it still belongs to the work of self-education. He who hopes to attain the full development of his mind or true manliness of character, without religious principle, is under a mistake. Knowledge is very important; but one sin will degrade you more than a great deal of ignorance. Sobriety, chastity, purity, and truth are elements of growth to the mind, not less than to the heart. They ennoble a man in this world, while they prepare him for the future; and these are the virtues which religion inculcates. It exalts us above all corrupting and impure associations, and therefore, if considered only as a means of self-improvement in the present time, it should never be neglected. The irreligious man is in danger of becoming a low-minded and selfish man, even if he avoids being wicked.

But I would not rest the cause of religion here. Not for a moment would I leave it upon so low a ground. It appeals to us and belongs to us, as immortal beings. It commands us to make the most of ourselves here, in mind, in heart, and in life, because we must soon pass from Time to Eternity, carrying with us the result of our conduct here. In such a view, how completely worthless do all earthly considerations seem? What matter whether we are rich or poor, learned or ignorant, so that we are rich in good works and wise unto salvation?

But a part of our duty towards God is to improve the talents committed to us, for the promotion of his glory and for usefulness among men. Infuse, therefore, into all your efforts for self-improvement a religious spirit. This will bestow dignity upon the employment, it will give steadfastness to your purpose and crown your efforts with success.

LECTURE IV.

TRANSGRESSION.

"Enter not into the path of the wicked, and go not in the way of evil men. Avoid it, pass not by it, turn from it, and pass away."—Prov. iv 14, 15.

NOT long ago, perhaps a year or more, I was accosted in the street by a man, whom at first I did not fully recognize. His voice, however, recalled him to my mind. I had not seen him for nearly two years, although we had both been living in the same city during all that time, and we had formerly been upon terms of intimate friendship. His hand was cold and tremulous; he was not intoxicated, but his step was unsteady, like that of an old man, and his form slightly bowed, as if under the weight of threescore years. His features were bloated, his eye dull and unsettled. He seemed unable to look steadily upon any object, and the expression of his face was like that of one suffering under some heavy care or some great disappointment that he was desirous to conceal. There was an effort to assume a hearty and cordial manner, and the grasp of the hand and the first words of greeting seemed like his manner of ten years before. But it was an effort that could not long be sustained. Assumed indifference and the evident sense of real mortification soon took its place. His dress was shabby and carelessly worn, showing that the world had not dealt kindly with him. He seemed glad to see me, shook my hand again and again, as if he had forgotten each time that he had done it before; promised to come to my house, which, however, he evidently did not intend to do; asked me to visit him, but although I promised it, he evidently supposed it would never be done, and seemed greatly relieved when the interview was ended. And so was I. But it left matter upon my mind which occupied me many hours after. His form kept coming back to me, an unbidden presence, reproaching me that I had not done more to save him from that sad condition. A few days afterward I went to see him at his room, and tried to renew our old acquaintance. I spoke to him earnestly and plainly, as I had often done before, and he promised, with tears in his eyes, that he would reform. Only a week afterward I again met him in the street, so intoxicated that he did not know me. And when two or three months had passed, I was called one day to see him on his dying bed, and then to follow him to an unhonored grave.

Was this the end to which he looked forward, when he first came to this city? Was this the natural and right conclusion of a youth full of promise, of a manhood which began with bright hopes and sanguine expectations? If, on the day when he left his father's house, "a younger son to go into a far country," the dream of such a future had visited him, — the vision of a premature old age, of years spent friendless and despised, of the death-bed in an alms-house and the burial at public charge, — if such a vision had come to him when he received his mother's blessing, or to her when she gave it, it would have been better for them both to be stricken down by the hand of death, than to look upon it. Yet the reality came, and that which would have been too fearful to think of became the history of his life.

And how did it come? By what avenues did the tempter find entrance into a heart rich in good affections, into a mind well stored with good and pious thoughts? I remember him now as he was, sixteen years ago, when he first came to this city. Among all whom I knew, I could not, perhaps, have selected one whose life seemed to give a more certain promise of an honorable and useful career. The glow of health was upon his cheek, his eye sparkled with the vigor of intelligence, his step was firm, his whole manner was that of one who had resolved to do a man's work manfully. He was then but little more than twenty years of age, fresh from all the good influences of a Christian home in a quiet Christian community, unstained by the world's corruptions, ignorant of life's temptations. But his resolutions were so strong and his opportunities so good, that there seemed as little danger for him as for any one. How terrible the change that fifteen years produced.

If I could trace that progress, step by step, —if I could show how it was that his virtuous resolutions began to yield, and the stain of corruption to spread upon his soul, it would be an instructive, although a sad narration. But the heart knoweth its own bitterness. We cannot enter into the hidden experience one of another. We cannot tell how the temptation comes, even to ourselves, and we often fail to recognize its presence until we have yielded to its power. The influences of evil are working in the heart, long before they come to outward observation. When we begin to see them, the ruin is too often already accomplished.

With regard to him of whom I have now spoken, I did not know when his steps began upon the downward road. He seemed to be prospering in business, for the first two or three years was found only in good company, and was evidently taking his place among men as a good and useful citizen. I have since thought, that perhaps his progress was so much more rapid than he had anticipated, and the position he held so much higher, that he was deceived into a false security. Perhaps he thought himself already removed from danger, and that he might safely yield to temptation, a little way, without fear of falling. Soon after, some reverses in business occurred which slightly embarrassed him, and some disappointments in social life which soured his disposition. The habit of occasional conviviality, formed in the time of prosperity, now brought a feeling of relief and daily became stronger. His place at church was more frequently left vacant, and his place at the bar-room more frequently filled. He was not himself aware of any danger, until, his business suffering more and more, he began to perceive that friends were falling away from him. Partly by the sense of shame, and partly by the feeling that he was unjustly dealt with, he was led to acquaintance with those who were, in character and social position, far beneath him. Their influence upon him was in every way bad. Some of them were those determined drinkers, those veterans in the ranks of intemperance, who are scarcely ever intoxicated, yet never sober, and who care very little how many others fall over the precipice, while they themselves remain in comparative safety. Under their influence his decline was rapid, and soon ended in vain tears of repentance, in sadness and despair.

It is a common story; a thing of every day's occurrence. Since I began to speak, if you have asked yourselves whose history it is, if you have tried to remember some one to whom it would apply, you have probably thought of many whose career, although not identically the same, has been equally sad.

Perhaps none of those whom I address know any thing of the person to whom I have referred; for the record of his name and of his burial-place has already passed from memory. But similar instances you have all known, or may see every day going on towards the fatal, the inevitable conclusion. In conversation with a friend a few days since, who is himself still a young man, he informed me that more than half of the companions with whom he began his active life, ten or twelve years since, have already come to a disgraceful death or to a dishonored and worthless life. Is it not dreadful to think of such things? Is it not enough to frighten a young man from his self-confident security, to see how many of those who have gone before him, in the very same path, have fallen never to rise again? Has he a safe-conduct from some higher power, by virtue of which he may go to the brink of ruin and return uninjured? Is it the mark of wisdom to risk every thing that makes life dear, health and friends, honor and usefulness, virtue and religion, self-respect and the favor of God, for the sake of those vulgar but enticing pleasures by which the young are so often betrayed? There is a warfare in which discretion is the better part of valor. Even if we gain the victory, we return without honor and without praise.

"Therefore enter not into the path of the wicked, and go not in the way of evil men; avoid it, pass not by it, turn from it, and pass away."

The paths which lead to ruin, although they gradually converge and become the broad and fatal "way that leadeth to destruction," are at first very various. The first departures from virtue are very slight, the first habits of sin seem to be in themselves scarcely sinful. There is some pleasant name by which they are called, some plausible excuse by which they are allowed. But by a little pains, we can mark the principal stages by which the downward progress is generally made.

First of all is the INTOXICATING CUP. With ninety-nine in a hundred, that is the beginning whose end is death. Those who begin with the strict rule of temperance, and adhere to it, seldom throw themselves away in sinful pursuits. Generally speaking, if the young man can secure himself in this bulwark of safety, all the enemies of his soul will be successfully resisted. His passions will remain under his own control, unless they are heated by wine, and his eye clear to see the things which are for his own good, unless clouded by the fumes of strong drink. But when he has put an enemy within his mouth to steal away his brains, influences which a child should be strong enough to resist become too strong for him, and he yields both body and soul to their power. He may think that it is very little he has taken, but a very little is enough to obscure the judgment of a young head and to pervert the desires of youthful blood. He may imagine that he was never more perfectly himself, his thoughts may seem to him more than usually clear, his step may have strength and buoyancy, there is just enough pleasant excitement to make his heart glad; but in all this he is prepared to say and do things from which perfect sobriety would shrink, and of which the soberness of to-morrow's thought will be ashamed.

Young men! I would warn you from that sparkling cup, — not only because it is a first step, which may lead you, as it has led, this very year now drawing to a close, fifty thousand in our own country, to a drunkard's grave, — but I warn you from it, because even from the very first it opens all the avenues of your heart to the temptations under which sin is committed. There is scarcely a sin against which you need a warning, so long as the blood flows equally in healthy channels; but when it is quickened by the liquid fire, the power of temptation is increased, while the strength to resist it is lessened. Sin puts on allurements which do not belong to it, and by which its deformity is concealed. The quiet pleasures of a virtuous life appear tame in comparison, and the disordered imagination fills the chambers of guilt with illusions of beauty, which the experience of guilt will soon destroy.

If it were, therefore, certain that you could indulge yourselves with safety, so far as the danger of intemperance is concerned, you would be exposing yourselves to other dangers equally as great. I appeal to you if this is not true. I ask you if you have not already gone far enough to know its truth? Let it be granted that it is impossible for you ever to become a drunkard; have you not already experienced that by the daily or occasional use of intoxicating drink you expose yourselves to many bad influences, from which you would otherwise escape, and commit many sins both in word and deed, which you would otherwise avoid? From what cause come wasted time and low companionship? What is it that betrays you into extravagance and foolish debt? By what means did you fall so easily into Sabbath-breaking and profanity? How did you learn to speak so lightly of religion and to laugh at the scruples of virtue? What influence has brought the sacredness of female innocence into contempt? and how has it come to pass that, instead of the nobler ambition of your early days, you are now so eager for pleasure, so greedy for excitement? Can you tell me? Have you thought of this? You feel very sure that you will never be a drunkard; but are you equally sure that the foundation of your virtue is not already sapped, that the springs of your moral and religious life are not already corrupted? Make the trial. Begin this day and continue for twelve months the plan of strict, absolute temperance, and you will be astonished to find how greatly the change of that one habit will change the tenor of your whole lives. You will have more time to yourselves; you will feel a greater desire of improvement; the deformity of vice will appear more plainly, and the excellence of virtue; your nobler ambition to be a useful and honored man will return; and before many months have passed, you will be astonished to see how far upon the road to ruin you had gone, and how difficult it is, even now, to retrace your steps. If you doubt my words, make a trial of them for your own sake. It can certainly do you no harm, and if at the end of twelve months you find that you are neither better nor wiser for the experiment, it will be easy to abandon it. But you will not find it so. Make the experiment for twelve months, and if you are capable of learning from experience, you will hold to it till the end of life.

This view of the subject is very important and needs to be carefully considered. Young men are every day ruined from the want of perceiving it. They convince themselves, as there is no difficulty in doing, that there is no danger of their ever becoming drunkards; and having done this, they excuse themselves in the habit of daily drinking, as if no other harm could come from it. A great and fatal mistake. From the very beginning it does harm. If it is only an occasional glass, if it is only the glow upon the cheek and the quickened pulse, produced by indulgence in wine at the supper-table of a friend, it is a wrong done, an injury inflicted. The perceptions of virtue are made dull, the rebukes of a tender conscience are silenced by such a habit from the very first. When the hour of perfect sobriety comes, the young man blushes to remember the words spoken and the acts of freedom of which he was guilty the night before. Consider this, I beg of you, and as you prize an unsullied conscience, let not the cup of intoxication come near your lips.

But how do you know that you are so safe? How do you know that you can walk in the path which leads to intemperance and yet never reach its end? Who gave you that safe-conduct, by power of which you may go to the brink of ruin, and looking over gaze into that fiery gulf and then return uninjured? *Uninjured, you cannot return.* That is impossible. But how do you know that you will return at all? Is it because you are so strong, — because you are always able to do what you say you will do? Men equally strong have fallen and are falling into that ruin every day. Is it because your motives to good conduct are so urgent on the one side, and because, on the other, you care so little for the intoxicating draught that you are sure you can give it up at any moment you please? It is only the delusion of Satan. Trust not to it. Your relish for that hateful cup is becoming stronger, although you may not know it. It may soon become so strong as to be a craving of your nature. It will be not only a sinful habit, but a physical disease. Your resolu-

tions become daily more weak and the strong will gradually loses its power. The motives for good conduct may continue or may grow stronger as the danger increases; but what are motives, to him whose feverish blood craves the drink which has already set him on fire? What to him are family and friends, or wife and children, or his own good name and self-respect, or health and life itself? What to him is the hope of heaven or the fear of hell? The drink which he craves he must have, and although he hates it, "he will seek it again."

Look at that man whose dress betokens that he is, or has been, a gentleman, and whose manners show that he is not yet quite brutalized. He staggers in the street, and because you have known him in his better days, you take his arm, and, half supporting him, go with him towards his home. You hear his maudlin talk and look into his lack-lustre eye, and wonder if that can be the same man whom you knew a few years ago in the pride of manhood, successful in business, beloved by his friends, honored by society. What motive was wanting to keep him in the right path? By what compulsion was he driven to a condition like this? You go on with him, for it is not far, until you are near his house; the effects of inebriation become stronger; he staggers so heavily that you can scarcely support him, and when he has come to his own door, it is with difficulty he stands. The door is opened, and what is it you then see? Do you talk of motives now? It is his wife and children who come forward to receive him. They know the whole truth; for it has been so many times before. His wife is still young and beautiful, but you see that her beauty, which you remember as it was a few years ago, is fading away under the influence of a wife's mortification and a mother's care. His daughter, already growing into womanhood, looks with half wonder and half disgust, and does what she is bidden to do to help her father. The younger children gather round, but quickly see that no caress is waiting for them there. And this is the drunkard's home. Do you talk of motives now? Do you not see that the habit of intemperance is like the robe with which Hercules was betrayed to clothe himself, and which he could not tear off, because it clung to him, a burning and a raging fire, until he was dead? It is but an allegory of drunkenness, and the strong man who subdues the Nemean lion is himself subdued, the victim of Intemperance.

But let your contempt be mingled with pity for him whom you left but now, in his miserable home. The day has been when, in the very agony of spirit, he knelt down and prayed to God, with vows that seemed registered in heaven, and with tears streaming from his eyes, while he promised that he would never again yield to temptation. You would have had hope for him then; but it lasted a few weeks, and the promises were broken. Merciful God! who knowest the weakness of our nature and the deceitfulness of our hearts, keep us away from temptation; save us from the trials which may be too strong for our virtue! Leave us not to our own devices, but save us with a strong hand, and guide us by thy Spirit in the way of everlasting life! And thou, young man, trifle not with your own soul. Pray that you may not be led into temptation. "Look not thou upon the wine when it is red, when it giveth its color in the cup, when it moveth itself aright. At the last it biteth like a serpent and stingeth like an adder."

But among those who hear me, are there not some whose minds suggest an answer to the appeal now made, and who therefore cannot feel its force? It is very well, they may say, and it is right for you as a minister of the Gospel to speak in this manner and advise us to keep out of temptation. We acknowledge the danger, and do not claim to be stronger than others who have fallen. You say that it is disgraceful for a young man to be a daily visitor at the bar-room, and we have often felt it to be so. But when we first went there, it was not of our own seeking. It was in performance of our duty. Our employers required it of us, or we knew that they expected it, and there was no way of avoiding it. Even now, it is a part of our regular employment to visit such places in search of customers, or to carry them there for the sake of keeping them in good humor and securing their patronage. If, therefore, the habit grows upon us, and we learn to continue it for our own sake, we do not well see how to avoid it. We must either run the risk or lose our places.

What shall we say to this? I wish that it could be denied, as a slander against the good name of this community, but it contains too much truth. I have known it to be true in many instances. There are some houses, so I am credibly informed, that have a contingent fund to defray the expenses incurred by their young men in this miserable pursuit of business. In others, the same thing is done in a less systematic way, but quite as effectually, and there are comparatively few in which it is absolutely forbidden. The young man is accounted valuable, and receives promotion, in proportion to his success in bringing customers and in selling to them large bills; although it is perfectly well known by what arts of persuasion it is accomplished. A merchant said to me a few days since, " If it goes on in this way, every house will need, not only a buying partner, and a selling partner, and a counting-room partner, but a drinking partner, to make it successful." If that were all, I would not complain so much. If men would do this work for themselves, it would only be another instance of a man's endangering his soul for money; but to send the young and inexperienced upon this bad errand, is a wrong beyond endurance. There can be no sufficient excuse for it. If the continuance of trade requires it, then is trade an accursed thing, in which no honorable man should engage. The competition which leads to it is unmanly, and the prosperity gained by it is disgrace. But we do not believe it. We confidently deny the necessity of resorting to such means, under any circumstances. Every respectable merchant should positively prohibit their use; and every respectable young man should positively refuse to be made the instrument of pandering to the vices of others, at the risk of his own virtue. Some temporary loss may be incurred, by adhering to such principles; but any loss is better than that of self-respect. Pardon me if I speak too plainly, and "he that hath ears to hear, let him hear."

Another way to ruin is found in the *violation of the Lord's day.* I spoke, last week, of the wasted Sunday as a hinderance to self-improvement. I speak of it now as a sin, the consequences of which are ruinous to the soul.

I am not what is commonly called a strict Sabbatarian. My ideas concerning the Lord's day are neither Jewish nor Puritan. "The Sabbath was made for man, not man for the Sabbath." Its superstitious observance either by the individual or by a community is not to be desired. Yet I have no doubt that the day was intended to be held sacred from the common uses of the week. If we are disposed to doubt this, experience and observation will prove it. If you devote it to your ordinary occupations, as a working day, or to the pursuit of pleasure, as a holiday, it will become to you a frequent occasion of sin, and both your mind and your character will suffer. This is partly because we need the refreshment of occasional rest from our ordinary pursuits, and one day in seven is not too much. It is needed equally by the mind and the body. Our affections need it to prevent their becoming dull or morbid; the judgment is more healthy and the thoughts more clear by a respite from labor. The eagerness of social ambition is restrained, and the comparative value of the different objects of pursuit more justly discerned.

This is the ordinary influence of the Lord's day, considered as a day of rest from our common labors, and without regard to its religious uses. Nor is there a community on the face of the earth which needs its restorative influence more than our own. I have sometimes thought, that if it were not for the Sabbath day, upon which we stop working, from motives of respectability if from no other, one half of us would go crazy, through the restless eagerness of our industry. In the breathing time which Sunday gives, we recover the exhausted strength, and return to our work with a spirit somewhat chastened and more free from unhealthy excitement. As business men, therefore, we lose nothing, but gain a great deal, by turning away from ordinary pursuits and resting from them one day in seven. There is no command of God's revealed word, which receives a more perfect confirmation from our own experience than this: "Remember the Sabbath day to keep it holy."

If you will consider it as giving time and opportunity for religious improvement, its importance still more fully appears. It is the time for meditation, for serious reading and for prayer. I do not mean that every hour of it must be so used, but that this use of the day should be prominent in our thoughts. None of us can safely dispense with it. Our religious progress will be slow, and our estrangement from God will become greater every day, unless some portion of the Sunday is regularly given to its religious uses. The young person who neglects these has no reason to be surprised to find himself becoming more and more irreligious. If he sets any value upon religion, if he does not wish to free himself altogether from the restraints which religion imposes, if he does not wish to make complete shipwreck of his religious hopes, then let him give a part of the Lord's day to the house of prayer, a part of it to his Bible, and a part to serious reflection. This is not asking too much; it may seem too much to those who have no higher object in life than to eat, drink, and be merry; but not to those who have any nobleness of character left, nor to those who believe that our chief duty here is to prepare ourselves for the future.

The profanation of the Lord's day to the purposes of amusement, seems almost to bring a special judgment upon those who are guilty of it. I do not mean by any outward punishment, but by the injury done to themselves, in their own moral and religious life. It generally precedes, if it does not mark, the decline of virtue and the growth of immorality. We may well be surprised at the extent to which this is true, until we look at the influences to which such a use of the day generally exposes us. It brings us into low associations. Sunday amusements are generally of a vulgar kind, and must be enjoyed, if at all, in vulgar companionship. Those who are seeking for a better respectability will not join in them. They are kept away by regard to their reputation, if not by higher principles If we seek them, therefore, our associates must be those who are more likely to relish vice than virtue, and whose influence upon us will be of the worst kind. The influences of the day, instead of being the best, become the most pernicious of the whole week; instead of being consecrated to God, it is made the occasion of sin. We have no reason, therefore, to wonder at the evil result. By familiarity with vulgar scenes, by friendship with vulgar associates, by separating ourselves from refined and religious society, we may go downward just as rapidly as we please.

Thus it is, that what is called Sabbath-breaking becomes so great a sin. Thus it often becomes the introduction to every vice, and to many young persons is the first step towards their ruin. It places them in a position where all the "fiery darts of the wicked" reach them. You may call the observance of the Lord's day a ritual observance, if you please, but it is inseparable from religion itself. It is inseparable from morality. If you neglect it, if you become a confirmed Sabbath-breaker, turning your feet away from the house of God, and devoting its hours to pleasure-seeking, your pleasures will soon become dissipation; even your respectability will be on the wane; your ideas of right and wrong will be more and more unsettled, and your soul itself is lost. I commend it, therefore, young men, to your serious consideration. Do not set it aside as a mere usage, which in itself is neither right nor wrong. Use it well, and it will become to you indeed the Lord's day, diffusing through the whole week a sanctifying influence, making your whole lives an acceptable service to Him. If you waste it or profane it, no one can measure the extent of the evil which may follow. Upon the Sabbath, therefore, even above all other days, remember "not to enter into the path of the wicked, not to go in the way of evil men. Avoid it, pass not by it, turn from it, and pass away."

Among the evil habits by which many young men are ruined, we must mention the *sin of gambling*. It is a subject upon which I have had almost no opportunity of observation. I must speak of it, therefore, with diffidence, because, so far as facts are concerned, my knowledge goes but little way. But I am told by others, that the evil to which we now refer exists among us to a great extent. I am told that it is a common habit among young men, both upon a small and a large scale. Occasionally I hear of those who lose more money in this way than they can afford; and at longer intervals, some marked instance comes before us, with a notoriety which ends in infamy, of those who have been betrayed by the gaming-table into dishonesty towards their employers and into their own ruin. We also hear sometimes, but are almost unable to believe it, that among the most respectable and influential men, gambling is a usage, and that those who, by their position in society, ought to set an example of the strictest morality, are exerting hereby a fatal influence. For such things, although they may be done in a corner, are sure to go abroad. They become a part of our moral atmosphere. It is breathed by the young man, whose principles are yet but imperfectly formed, and taints his moral nature. The necessity of virtue seems less urgent, the hideousness of vice becomes less hateful. The responsibility which rests upon those who stand at the head of society, by whatever cause they are placed there, cannot be exaggerated. They would do well to consider it more maturely. If not for their own sake, then for the sake of those who look to them as an example, and in whose eyes they are making wickedness respectable, they should discountenance this, as well as every otner form of social iniquity.

But our business at present is with the

young themselves; with those whose visits to the gambling-table have as yet been few, and who have not yet experienced its worst influence. If the habit is already confirmed, they are probably beyond the reach of our influence; for of all sinful habits, there is none whose enticements are so alluring to those who have taken the first step, none which binds around its votary cords more difficult to be broken. We address ourselves also to those by whom the first step has not yet been taken. Upon them, chiefly, an influence may be exerted. With all the earnestness we are capable of using, we implore them to keep away from the gaming-table. As they love their souls, as they value their peace of mind, yes, as they prize their common respectability in the world, let them keep away.

The evils of gambling are so many, that I scarcely know how to enumerate them. First, and unavoidably, it leads the young man into the worst of company. The game of chance is a complete leveller. For a time there may be a vain effort of exclusiveness, but it will not continue long. Very soon he is upon terms of intimacy with those whom he despises, and who despise or hate him in return. Again, from the very first, an unhealthy excitement is produced, not so much an excitement as a fever of the mind. It often grows to a delirium, under which all self-control is lost, an intoxication worse than that of drunkenness itself. It is at such times that one is betrayed into dishonesty, when he stakes upon the turn of a card money which he must dishonestly steal, before he can honorably pay He scarcely knows what he is doing; when it is done, he is as much astonished as we are to hear of it; but it is then too late. A step taken upon that road is followed by another and another, until discovery and ruin overtake him.

To the beginner at the gaming-table, the intoxicating cup is always made an adjunct of the evil, and thus one temptation is increased by the other. The confirmed gambler, indeed, is shrewd enough to keep himself sober. If he drinks freely, it is because he has inured himself by long habit, so that he does not feel its influence; but generally, he takes only enough to lead others beyond their depth. A confirmed gambler, therefore, is seldom a drunkard. But with the tyro it is quite different. He lacks nerve for his new employment. He feels a little ashamed of himself; he is acting a part which he is not used to; he feels timid and hesitates; and for all such feelings, wine is a panacea; or, by some beverage more ingeniously contrived, he is soon brought to a degree of self-confidence which makes him feel quite at home. How great does the peril now become! He goes downward at an increasing pace. Late in the evening, he returns home with a feverish brain, but with a heart already heavy as lead, and on the morrow curses the day on which he was born.

Again, the habit of gambling, whether on a large or small scale, develops the worst feelings of a man's nature. It makes him cold and selfish and distrustful. He learns to hate those whom he calls his friends, for their gain is continually his own loss. He regards them with suspicion, accuses them of unfairness, thinks that they are overreaching him and endeavors to overreach them in return. Under such a discipline all frankness of character gives way; all scrupulousness of conscience disappears; mean and tricky subterfuges are resorted to, and each one becomes guilty of that of which he suspects the other. A great deal is said about debts of honor, but the principal debt is that incurred in one's own soul by the loss of honor itself.

["The *purchase of lottery tickets* is one of the worst species of gambling which any man or woman ever engaged in. It has all the temptations and excitements, and offers more inducements, than the Faro-bank or the Roulette-table. There are but few persons who have engaged in the purchase of lottery tickets that have not continued to pursue it, and with many it becomes a passion as fearful as any in the catalogue. It is tempting, because it requires but a small sum to commence, and the drawing of one or two numbers is sufficient to lure the victim on. The excitement is great, from the amount of gain in prospect, and the duration of the suspense. At the gambling-table, the money is down, the stake must bear some proportion to the amount to be won, and a few turns of the cards, or throws of the dice, decide it. But not so in this lottery business. A dollar, or a few dollars, invested in lottery tickets, will, if successful, enrich the holder with as many or more thousands. From the moment of the purchase until the announcement of the result of the drawing, he lives in a state of painful and improper excitement. At one moment, golden visions dance before the distempered brain, and fancy pictures the possession of thousands; the next, all is lost, and the holder is the victim of every species of ill-fate and misfortune.

"There are two classes of the community who are peculiarly susceptible to the influence of this evil excitement, and upon whom the reports of special good fortune, on the part of a few, are calculated to have a most pernicious influence. They are the young, and females. They are both desirous of the enjoyment of wealth, independence, and fortunes. They are susceptible of the influence which such reports carry with them. They can see no reason why they may not be as lucky as anybody else, and, once in the vortex, they are ruined. A failure, or partial success, but induces further trials; and thus they go on, step by step, until their money is exhausted, their honor and every thing sacrificed to a depraved and unreasonable passion."*]

In what I am now saying, I again acknowledge that I speak from theory more than observation. In these departments of life, my opportunities of observing are very small. But the little I have seen, interpreted under the general principles of human nature, justifies all that has been said. If so, my appeal cannot be too earnestly made. Keep away

---

* The above extract is taken from the leading editorial of the St. Louis Republican, Nov. 20, and is here introduced, although not in the Lecture delivered, as indispensable to the subject discussed.

from the gambling-table. Nay, keep away from the places where it is spread. Do not by your presence there give countenance to that great iniquity. Do not, for the sake of a transient pleasure, suffer your name to be enrolled among those who are guilty of this sin. Even if you refrain from it yourself, you are giving your patronage to those who live by it, and you are thereby committing a grave and serious offence against society. Do not answer, that you must have some amusement. It is not so needful, that you must commit sin or endanger your virtue in its pursuit. Let your hearts be set upon something better than amusement, upon self-improvement and a useful life, and you will find ways of recreation without entering "upon the path of the wicked, or going in the way of evil men."

My time is already more than exhausted, and with it my own strength, and I fear your patience. Yet there is one other topic upon which I must speak, before closing. It is a subject the most difficult of all, requiring at the same time plainness and delicacy in its treatment. I must trust to your own thoughts to supply my deficiency; and to your own love of virtue, that a right direction to your thoughts may be given

> "So dear to Heaven is saintly CHASTITY,
> That, when a soul is found sincerely so,
> A thousand liveried angels lackey her,
> Driving far off each thing of sin and guilt;
> . . . . . But when lust,
> By unchaste looks, loose gestures, and foul talk,
> But most by lewd and lavish act of sin,
> Lets in defilement to the inward parts,
> The soul grows clotted by contagion,
> Embodies and imbrutes, till she quite lose
> The divine property of her first being."

When speaking upon the same subject, Solomon asks, "Can a man take fire in his bosom, and his clothes not be burnt? Can one go upon hot coals, and his feet not be burnt?" Again the Apostle Paul says, "Know ye not that your bodies are the members of Christ? Shall I then take the members of Christ, and make them the members of a harlot? God forbid! What, know ye not that your body is the temple of the Holy Spirit which is in you, which ye have of God, and ye are not your own? If any man defile the temple of God, him shall God destroy; for the temple of God is holy; which temple ye are." In hearing such words, we feel that our bodies are sacred, and that we have no right to profane them by the defilement of sin. We should avoid impurity of thought and of action, as we avoid contagion and death. No grave for the soul can be dug so deep, as that in which it is buried by licentiousness.

Of all the influences in society, calculated to purify and elevate man's character, that of virtuous and well-educated women is perhaps the strongest. From the hallowed precincts of the domestic circle, it drives away all sinful pleasure; in the intercourse of social life, it makes virtue attractive and sin hateful. It touches the soul to its gentler issues, and bestows a grace upon whatever is noble in human life. An essential part of the education of a young man is in woman's society. He needs it as much as he needs the education of books, and its neglect is equally pernicious. Every one knows that it is a good trait in a young man, to be fond of ladies' society. I do not mean, to become what is technically called a ladies' man, which is very frequently another term for foppishness and effeminacy, and by which many make themselves objects of just contempt; but I mean that he who can enjoy the refined pleasure which comes from female society is not likely to enjoy himself in the haunts of dissipation.

But in proportion as she exerts a good and purifying influence when well educated and virtuous, her influence becomes pernicious if her character is perverted. When frivolous or heartless, she turns many from good; when wicked, she is the most successful minister of ruin. The best things perverted, become the worst. Take from the air we breathe one of its component parts, and a single breath of it causes death. Take from woman's character her love and practice of virtue, and her presence becomes death to the soul. He who betrays her from her innocence is not less hateful in the eyes of God, than the serpent who brought sin into Paradise. He who is upon terms of friendship with her after she is betrayed, unless for the purpose of restoring her to virtue, is helping her to sink lower in her degradation, and himself goes down with her to the gates of hell.

How does such an one dare to come from the scenes of iniquity to the society of the pure and good? How does he dare to touch the hand of her whose face expresses the beauty of innocence? As when Satan stood among the sons of God, we say to him, "*Whence* comest thou," and what place have you here? His own sense of shame should keep him away; or if he comes, he should be driven away with scorn. I know that it is in part woman's own fault, for very often when she knows full well whence he cometh, she welcomes him with smiles; but in doing so she is a traitor to her own sex, and stains her own purity. It is disgraceful to society that men, for whose description every English word is too vulgar, and over whose conduct a veil is thrown by calling them "roués," should be admitted even in the highest circles upon equal terms, yes, and often upon better terms, with honest and honorable men.

Young men! I would speak to you upon this subject even more earnestly, if I dared. I commend it to your own thoughts. He who loses his respect for woman and his veneration for woman's virtue, is sinking very fast; he is travelling very rapidly towards ruin. I appeal to each one of you, therefore, by the love which you bear to your own mother, or by the sacredness of her memory, by the tender affection which you feel for your own sisters, and by the indignation which would fill your hearts, if any one were to approach them with an impure word or look, — I appeal to you by the respect which you cannot help feeling for the innocence and purity of womanhood, — to keep your own purity of character and to avoid this worst contamination of sin.

Alas! how many are the dangers that threaten you! What watchfulness, what energy of purpose, do you need? The ground upon which you stand is enchanted. Perils and snares are around you.

> "Beware of all, guard every part,
> But most, the traitor in your heart."

"Wherewithal shall the young man cleanse his way? by taking heed thereto, according to Thy word. Enter not into the path of the wicked, and go not in the way of evil men. Avoid it; pass not by it: turn from it, and pass away."

LECTURE V.

THE WAYS OF WISDOM.

"And when he came to himself, he said, I will arise and go to my father, and will say unto him, Father, I have sinned against Heaven, and before thee. And he arose, and came to his father." — Luke xv. 17, 18, 20.

From my choice of these words as a text, it might naturally be supposed that I intend to speak only of those who have wandered far from the right path, and whose danger is already imminent. The young man in the parable "went to a far country," by which is indicated the degree of his iniquity; his living was quite wasted, and all his means of self-support quite gone, before he came to himself. Then, when his unworthiness was complete, and there was no other to whom he could turn, he said, "I will arise and go to my father"; scarcely hoping indeed to be received, but having no other hope to save him from despair.

How perfectly true to nature, when all other friends deserted him, that he turns himself to the home of his childhood, seeking forgiveness first from those whom he has most injured! It is the father's house and the mother's love, to which we turn as a sure haven of rest, when the world treats us unkindly. It is there that we are most sure to find acceptance, however great our ill-desert. Although sinful and degraded, friendless and outcast, we are sure of a welcome there. Nor is there a pang which the world's worst treatment can inflict so severe as this thought, that in spite of all our errors, in spite of all our ingratitude, in spite of all our heartless disobedience, a welcome is ready for us there, whenever we will return; that a fond mother will find excuses for us through the greatness of her love, and hope for us through the greatness of her faith; that the father, although he may seem more stern, is ready, whenever he sees us returning, to come out and meet the penitent, "to fall upon his neck and kiss him." Such is a parent's love; so great is a parent's forbearance. If it had not been for his confidence in this, must there not have been times when the weight of his sins would have crushed the prodigal, when the degree of his unworthiness would have driven him to despair? But the remembrance of that love which no ill-desert could estrange awakened hope for himself, and drew him back again to the paths of virtue.

How precious, therefore, to our souls, should be that Gospel which reveals the ALMIGHTY GOD, whom we have offended, as the Father who is in Heaven! What hopes are excited by that word, while at the same time the greatness of our sin is made more fully to appear! For in proportion to the long-suffering of those whom we offend is our wickedness in offending them. But still that precious hope returns, and if He whom we have chiefly offended is most ready to forgive, we will yet arise and go to our Father, and say unto him, "Father, we have sinned against Heaven, and before thee."

But need we wait until we have wandered so far? May we not feel the truth of all I have said, even when our steps have gone but a little way from the Father's house? Must we wait until the soul is buried under sin before we attempt to rise from it? Must he who feels the power of disease taking hold upon him wait until the whole body is corrupted, and the strength nearly gone, before he appeals to the physician? What then must be the consequence, but fatal disease and death? If I understand the Scriptures, salvation is needed by those who have gone but a little way in sin, as well as by those who are reaching its furthest limit. The peril may not seem to be as great, but the saving power is equally needed. In both cases, the principle of life is wrong, and a radical change is therefore required.

The weeds which are springing up in a cultivated garden may seem to be insignificant and a few moments' care would remove them; but small as they now are, they contain already the elements of mischief. Give them time to grow, and it is all they need. Their roots strike deeper, they gather to their own pernicious uses the strength of the soil; they grow up rapidly, overshadowing and stunting the growth of the worthier plant, and coming to an early maturity, they scatter the seeds of increasing mischief. The wind disperses them abroad, until, in a few years, the whole garden has lost its fruitfulness, and the neighboring fields are also ruined. Then, if you would eradicate those weeds, which a year ago were so insignificant, you must strike the plough deep and turn their roots up to the light of heaven; and years of patient industry will be needed before you rid yourselves of the evil. Is it not better to pull them up when they are but few, and their hold upon the soil feeble? They are evil now, is it not better to prevent them from becoming the parent of greater evil? But remember that, whenever you take them in hand, precisely the same process is needed for their effectual removal. You may pull them up as with your fingers, or the ploughshare may be required for the work; but, in either case, they must be pulled up. To trample upon them or to cut them down will not do; the root is still there and will spring up again. To scatter good seed among them is not enough; for there is danger that the weeds will grow up fastest, and "choke the good seed," even as it has been from the beginning. It may be only the sin of occasional Sabbath-breaking; it may be only that slight degree of dissipation which is softened by the name of wildness or youthful folly; it may be only the habit of profanity, by which no great harm is intended, and of which, although we may acknowledge that it is a proof of bad manners, we are not willing to acknowledge that it is an evidence of a bad heart; or it may be any other of those thousand forms in which sin makes its first entrance into the unguarded heart; but the sentence is still the same, — they must be rooted out, they must be pulled up from the soil, if we would secure our safety.

That little fire which sin is kindling in the soul may at first seem only to diffuse a gentle warmth, and to bestow upon all the faculties an increased vigor; but see to it, or it will become a raging and tormenting flame, consuming even your desire of goodness. It is better to put it out. Extinguish it while you can. It is an easy work now, but by and by nothing but the miracles of God's love can enable you to accomplish it.

There is something very pleasant, very encouraging, in the Scriptural expression, "when he came to himself." It recognizes the fact that there is a better nature within us than that which sin develops. We are not wholly of the earth, a part is also from heaven; as it is written, "God created man and made him in his own image." It is true, that by our own sinfulness, and through the wicked inventions of the world, his image is partially effaced, or covered over by so thick a veil of the earth's pollutions, that it is scarcely discerned; but yet it remains there, never completely lost, never hidden beyond the hope of being again restored. That heavenly image is the better self. It is of God, yet it is our own. By virtue of it, we claim alliance with God, and brotherhood with Christ. If it were utterly lost, salvation would be impossible. The greatest sinner whom Christ ever redeemed, when he arises from the deadly sleep and awakens to righteousness, does but come to himself. In the farthest land, destitute and hungry, feeding the swine which belong to a stranger, desiring to share with them in their food, friendless and utterly degraded, he says, I will arise; he comes to himself, and at the same time looks upward to his God. We know how deadly are the sins of which the human soul is capable. We know how fearful its wickedness becomes. We know its waywardness, its ingratitude, its rebellion against God. But we thank God that there is still a better self to which the sinner may return. O man, my brother, in the very hopelessness of iniquity does not that thought bring hope? Thou art not all debased; thou art not yet utterly depraved; scarred and disfigured, changed from all the beauty which was once thine own, something of the Divine lineaments yet remains in thy soul. There is yet a better self. Return to it; in the strength which God will give, if you ask him, say, "I will arise and go to my Father."

But, we again ask, why should we wait until the hour of extreme want, before we return to the Father's house? Why should we wait until our best affections are seared, and the purity of our souls quite lost, and our capacity for improvement impaired, before we recognize our true good? Do we need that the lesson should be so severely taught, before we will learn it? Should it not be enough to know that the road leads in a wrong direction, to induce us to leave it? Must we go to the very end, and only when ruin stares us in the face be willing to retrace our steps? Then we shall return, if at all, way-worn and haggard, weary of the world, wounded in the conflict with sin, with hearts so full of sadness that we can scarcely find room for rejoicing, and even the hope of God's mercy will be mingled with fears. Now we are choosing the direction of life, and it requires only one strong resolution, one earnest prayer, to make the direction right.

Or if we have already gone a little way in the wrong path, the vigor of youth and the strength of manhood remain, and although some time has been lost, we may yet redeem it; although some stain has been brought upon our souls, the tears of repentance will quickly wash it off, and we shall be restored to self-respect and virtue.

Consider this, young men, and ponder these words with care. If I appeal to you so earnestly, it is not because I suppose that you have already reached that far country of deadly sin and remorse, but that you may save yourselves from it.

I would show you that this flowery path, in which you are walking, is wrong in its direction, although pleasant for the time. Is there not a struggle already going on in your hearts, between the higher and lower principles of your nature? It is the great conflict, the struggle of life and death. Let the whole energy of a strong will be thrown into it, and the victory will be for God and your own souls. Wait not until evil has become the habit of your lives, a second nature scarcely to be changed; but prevent the formation of sinful habits, now while it can be so easily done. Keep yourselves from bad influences, surround yourselves with the safeguards of virtue. It is often better to avoid temptation than to overcome it. The sight of evil sometimes leaves in the mind thoughts and images, which are better not to be there. It is for this reason that I speak so earnestly, as if it were, as I believe it is, a matter of infinite moment. Experience and observation both tell us, that the elements of the same nature are in us all. He that has gone farthest from his God went one step at a time, as perhaps we are going now. The lowest degradation of the worst man living is only the result of the same wayward tendencies, to which we are perhaps sometimes yielding; of the same bad passions, which we perhaps sometimes indulge. I know that the evil has not yet come in its full force, but honestly speaking, do we not discern its possibility? Have we not had enough experience of evil in our own hearts, have we not actually done enough in our own lives, to justify the fear of its indefinite increase? What then is the course of wisdom? Is it not to stop now while it is easy to stop? Is it not to change the direction of life, before life itself is almost wasted?

A mistake is often made in thinking of salvation as something which belongs to the future world alone, and not at all to the present. Life is represented as if it were only a preparation for that beyond the grave. We forget that it has its own absolute duties. It should have in itself a completeness; it should be in itself a service of God. We have a work to do for ourselves, for each other, and for the glory of God, which must be done here. Even if we were sure of ultimate salvation, the neglect of this present work is a great evil and a great sin. It is a wrong committed against God, against humanity against our own souls. Even if we escape from its worst consequences by repentance before we die, it is a wrong in itself, which it is the part of wisdom to avoid. I shall ask you, therefore, in what remains of my present discourse, to look at the duties of life from this point of view. Let us consider our life here, not as being only a preparation for the future, but as being something in itself. Its duties, its relations, its joys and sorrows, its virtues and sins, are a present reality. To do our part here well and manfully, is something worth doing. As, therefore, with reference to the future life and to the great salvation, we speak of the "means of grace," by which redemption is obtained; so, with reference to the present life, we speak of the means of improvement, the human safeguards of virtue. These must be used, if we would make the best of our own faculties and of life itself. We must exercise good sense in our plans of life, and place ourselves under the influences which favor goodness and discourage sin. Some of these influences we shall now consider.

The first condition of good health is to breathe a good atmosphere. If with every breath the seeds of disease are brought to the lungs or the heart, the body will soon show the baneful effect, in the loss of its vigor and strength. The influence may be very subtle, but it is all the more irresistible. So in the formation of character, — for the preservation of health to the mind and the affections, to maintain the purity of our moral nature, the moral atmosphere must be pure. The associations into which we are daily brought must be favorable to virtue. The society in which we daily live must be of a kind to elevate the character.

It is an old proverb, that "a man is known by *the company he keeps*." This is true, for two reasons. First, because, as like seeks like, our real tendencies are shown by the sort of company we enjoy. If it is vulgar and dissipated, our seeking it proves that we have a relish for vulgarity and dissipation. The man of pure feeling and refined taste does not feel at home in such companionship; it gives him no pleasure and he avoids it, as he would avoid any thing else disagreeable. When, therefore, we see a person frequently in such company, it is a fair and just inference that he is there because he likes it, and therefore that he is himself of the same sort. The proverb is true for another reason. A man is known by the company he keeps, because, however different from it he may be at first, he will gradually become like it, almost whether he will or no. We are moulded by the society in which we live, more than by any other influence. It is the atmosphere by which we are surrounded, it is the breath which sustains life itself. The good man, who goes among the wicked for the purpose of instructing and reclaiming them to the path of virtue, needs to be careful, lest his own moral nature become tainted by the contact. Even in his endeavors to cure them, as sometimes with the physician who cures disease, while he is engaged in his work of mercy the contagion may reach his own heart. Even under such circumstances, we need the disinfectant of God's grace to secure us from evil. But when we enter into wicked or irreligious society for the sake of its companionship; when we seek our friends there in the enjoyment of social intercourse; however pure we may be at our entrance, our doom is already sealed, and the loss of innocence and virtue is the unavoidable result.

How can we retain our veneration for God and for his glorious majesty, if our ears are every moment filled with the profanation of his name? How can we think of Christ as our Redeemer, when the name of Jesus is a by-word, coupled with every stale jest, and bandied about, in anger or in sport, by those whom he died to save? How can we keep any sacredness of thought, any respect for religion, — the strong hope of heaven or the fear of hell, — if every thing sacred is made the subject of ridicule, or spoken of with careless contempt, by those with whom we have the daily intercourse of friendship? How can we keep before us the necessity of virtue, the infinite value of the soul, the infinite evil of sin, if we are daily living among those who suffer no scruples of virtue to interfere with their pleasures, and who can always find an excuse for sin if it is profitable? Let your own observation of the world, let your own experience of life, answer. The instances are so few, where young men have placed themselves under the influence of bad companionship and escaped its contamination, that they scarcely need to be considered. They are exceptions to a rule which is almost universal. The young man may deceive himself. At first, he may suppose that his principles are not corrupted; that he enjoys the companionship, its laughter and its fun, without partaking of its evil spirit. He may flatter himself that the evil which he hears and sees, only makes him love virtue more; but he is only deceiving himself. When the Apostle Paul speaks of wicked men and their sins, he thus describes them: "Who not only do such things, but have pleasure in them that do them." To take pleasure in the company of the wicked, is but one step from being wicked ourselves. As a natural and almost inevitable consequence, the word of blasphemy will soon come from our own lips; the cup of intoxication will soon be in our own hands; the cards and the dice will bring the fever to our hearts; and the paths of dissipation will become as familiar to our feet, as they are to those of our companions. Is not this the natural result? According to the laws of the human mind, by the natural working of our affections, ought we not to expect it? Is it not the actual result, of which your own observation could bring a hundred proofs, and to which your own experience is perhaps adding one proof more?

We again say that the society in which we live is the moral atmosphere we breathe. If it is bad, there is but one way of escaping its bad influence, — namely, to change it. A method of cure which requires strong resolution, but there is no other. Change it, if need be, by withdrawal at first from all society, and gradually obtain the friendship of those whom you can respect, instead. The change may require resolution, and will also be attended with difficulties. Those whom you leave will place every obstruction in your way; but if you act, not in a self-righteous and hypocritical manner, but with frankness and gentlemanly courtesy, even your old companions will respect you more, and some of them, perhaps, accompany you in the better path. I am inclined to think that whole companies of young men sometimes continue in the road to ruin, only for the want of two or three in their number, who have resolution enough to say, "We will stop; we will go no farther; we will abandon this course of life; we will live as gentlemen and Christians ought to live." Let a few say this, quietly but firmly, and the hearts of many will respond. The truth is, that all have been half ashamed of themselves for a long time, and have been hurried forward by each other's example, each one wanting the resolution, rather than the disposition, to stop. Let that resolution be shown by a few, and others will be strengthened thereby, and perhaps the progress of all will be stayed. But whether such a result follow or not, the duty of the individual is the same. If he feels within himself the strength to stop, let him use it. Let him withdraw from the associations in which his own virtue is corrupted and in which he is corrupting the virtue of others. It is not a matter of expediency only; it is not for the sake of respectability alone, or of obtaining a better position in society, although this would be in itself motive enough to a thoughtful man; but it is the question of virtue or vice; it is the alternative between a life well spent or utterly lost.

We say, therefore, to the young man who has been brought, either by circumstances beyond his control or by his own choice, into the society of uneducated or vulgar or dissipated companions, that the sooner he frees himself from such influences the better, and that he must free himself soon, or he will be under the servitude of sin for ever. Still more earnestly we say to those who have not yet entered into such companionship, keep away from it as you would avoid the contagion of disease, the corruption of iniquity. It may have its allurements; its fascinations may be many to the young and thoughtless; the sin committed may at first seem small; but it is the companionship itself that brings the danger, and as you value the purity, nay, the salvation of your souls, it should be avoided. So long as we are in the company of the good, goodness is easy. Choose your companions well, among those who have correct views of life, who respect religion, who avoid the paths of dissipation, and a virtuous life will be so pleasant that you will desire no other. This is the great safeguard of virtue. The best of us are not strong enough to dispense with it; to the young and inexperienced it is every thing. Particularly in their unguarded and leisure hours, when they seek for amusement and recreation from toil, let the companionship in which they share be good. For, as the unwholesome air is most fatal to the body when asleep, so is the contagion of bad example most fatal, when the mind rests from its serious occupations, and throws itself, in unguarded repose, upon the influences which surround it. Then it is that the excellence of virtue or the deceitfulness of sin prevails over us, according to the company in which we are. We should select it, therefore, with such views, that, while we gain refreshment for the mind, our love of virtue may be strengthened, our tastes refined, and our desires of goodness confirmed.

The kindness with which you have thus far heard me, and upon which I have already encroached by unusual plainness of speech, will perhaps allow me to speak of another subject, upon which judicious advice is sometimes needed. One of the best rules for the preservation of virtue, and for keeping ourselves away from temptation, is to avoid extravagance, to keep *out of debt.* Economy is a word which, to the majority of young persons, conveys the idea of meanness. It should rather convey the idea of independence. We would not check the youthful feeling of generosity. We would be among the last to inculcate meanness, nor is there any one to whom a niggardly and parsimonious young man is more disagreeable than to me. Such a character in the young is against nature.

At first sight, extravagance itself seems more excusable. But on the other hand, extravagance is a sort of dishonesty; to live beyond one's income often degenerates into the worst meanness; to owe money that we cannot pay, drives one to subterfuges and unmanly evasions, of which no one can help being ashamed. Debt is a kind of servitude, under which it is hard to retain the more manly virtues of freedom. Under its influence, our own self-respect is very apt to be diminished. It is mortifying to acknowledge even to ourselves that there are men whom we are almost afraid to meet, and to whom we have given the right to treat us in a manner to hurt our feelings. The creditor who demands payment, and the debtor who is unable to make it, are seldom upon equal terms.

There is no rule, therefore, more important in maintaining independence of feeling and a nice sense of honor, than to live within one's means, so that we may have an answer to give to every one who says, "Pay me that thou owest." I have known many young persons, whose prospects in life have been ruined by neglect of this rule. Debts, thoughtlessly incurred, give food for anxious thought afterward, and it is astonishing how great an effect upon the whole character is produced. The young man suffering under this sort of anxiety, eager for an increase of income, discontented with what he now receives, uneasy lest his embarrassment may be known, fearful of being dunned, is in no state of mind for self-improvement. When alone, he is too nervous to read, when in company too restless for its enjoyment. The tone of his mind becomes unhealthy and his mode of life careless. On the other hand, the feeling that he does not depend upon the favor of any one, that he is always in a position to change his place, if unjustly treated, and that he is not obliged to seek any man's favor by unworthy stooping, produces a feeling of self-respect, which will save him from a great deal of folly.

Another safeguard of virtue is found in *good books*. By surrounding ourselves with them, and making ourselves familiar with them as with beloved companions, we take an effectual means of self-improvement; we place ourselves beyond the reach of many temptations; we secure a fund of enjoyment, rich and unfailing. It is a source of delight, of rational happiness, which can never be exhausted, but still becomes greater, and is prized more and more to the end of life. He who loves reading, and has books within his reach, is an independent man, be he rich or poor. Every volume he opens is a cordial friend, whose hand he grasps and whose countenance towards him does not change.

We lose ourselves from the vexations of life, we retire from its cares, we forget its disappointments; even its bereavements are softened to our hearts, when we thus ponder the wisdom of the dead, or receive the quickening thoughts of the living. How sacred, how blessed, is that intercourse! how ennobling the companionship, when we stand with Milton, and Socrates, and Shakspeare, and Homer, and Addison, and Johnson, and Schiller, and Goethe, and all the worthies of every land and every age, from MOSES, the great lawgiver, and DAVID, the greatest poet, to our own WEBSTER and BRYANT. When they are all around us, with all their best thoughts, their sagest instruction; with the gay sparkling of fancy, and wit provoking laughter until it comes with tears; or with images of sorrow and pathetic tenderness, which make our hearts almost bleed, yet with not an unpleasing sadness; in such companionship, though alone, how glorious society we enjoy! Who could ask any thing of the world when the treasure of such riches is his own?

Who can enjoy the society of the vulgar, or enter upon scenes of dissipation, when he has learned to enjoy pleasures so refined, in company so select and beautiful?

The love which the scholar feels for his books, none but a scholar can understand; but every one who diligently seeks for self-improvement must learn something of it from his own experience, or his progress will be slow. The taste for reading is one of the surest marks of an improving mind and a virtuous character. But it will not come of itself. At first it must be cultivated with diligence, as we would perform any other duty. Other engagements will seem more attractive, and we shall sometimes take up our books with a feeling of weariness, as an irksome task; but the habit will soon be formed. As the mind gains knowledge, we shall love the sources from which knowledge comes.

We need offer no argument to show that to the individual the habit is invaluable; to be a reading man is, generally speaking, to be a moral man and a useful citizen. To a community it is equally important; for to be an enlightened community and a reading community are but two expressions for the same thing. I would not lay so much stress upon this point, having already spoken of it once before in these lectures, but because I think that this is the respect in which, as a community, we are most deficient. Our young men need to have their attention turned away from mere amusement, to the higher pleasure which reading affords. They need more of that education and refinement, which books alone can give. No other human influence can do more than this to check the growth of intemperance and to elevate the moral standing of this city. If I had it in my power to close every bar-room and place of wickedness, and to prohibit the sale of intoxicating drink by law, I should probably exercise the power with great gladness; but not one half the good would be thereby accomplished, nor would it be half so well done, as by giving to all our young men so great a taste for reading, that they would lose the taste for dissipation. If we could thus take away the occupants of our splendid saloons, their splendor would soon fade away.

It is for this reason that we look with so great pride upon the growth of an institution whose express object is to cultivate the taste for reading among us, and to provide means for its exercise. I refer to the Mercantile Library Association. It is a good beginning and promises well for the future. We would place it next to the institutions of religion itself, as a means of promoting virtue and discouraging vice. We mention it in this connection for another reason also; because it is not only intended chiefly for the benefit of our young men, but because it is chiefly the work of our young men themselves. It is true, indeed, that they have received from the older part of the community, efficient and indispensable aid; but the laboring oar has been in the hands of young men themselves, or of those who are but just passing into the years of middle life. More than half of its annual subscribers are young men, who are not themselves yet established in business. Its growing favor in this community is, therefore, one of the best evidences of improvement. Its library, although not large, is well selected, and, being easily accessible to young men, offers to them means of self-improvement and rational enjoyment, which no young man is wise to neglect. We hope that the spacious rooms which will soon be ready for its use will not be too large for the accommodation of those who desire to avail themselves of its privileges.

Will you also indulge me if I take this opportunity of paying a tribute to the memory of one, of whose death, in a distant land, we have recently heard. Although a young man, he was among the early friends of the institution just now named, and, at the time of his leaving this city, one of its directors. Himself a beginner in life, he gave what is often better than money, his time and personal attention to its interests. I refer to THEODORE CLARK. From his boyhood I knew him well, and watched over him in his youth and early manhood, not only as his pastor, but as his friend. His death is to me a personal grief, and to this church, of which he was a valued member, an irreparable loss. Although he had removed for the time to a distant home, his place here did not seem to be vacant, until now. The tears which fall to his memory are those of sincere sorrow, and the tribute of respect now paid is also the tribute of affection.

How mysterious are those dispensations of Providence, by which the young and useful are taken away in the beginning of their career! But the dealings of God are not measured by the wisdom of men. Death knows no distinction either of age or place. However young and strong, the warning is equally to us all. Be ye ready also, for in a day and hour when ye think not, the Lord cometh. Are we ready now? If death were to call us hence to-day or to-morrow, could we obey the summons without fear? He who lives as he ought is always prepared to die. "Rejoice, O young man, in thy youth," saith the Scripture, "and let thy heart cheer thee, in the days of thy youth; but know thou, that for all these things God shall bring thee into judgment." Therefore, "fear God and keep his commandments, for this is the whole duty of man."

LECTURE VI.

RELIGION

"I beseech you therefore, brethren, by the mercies of God, that ye present your bodies a living sacrifice, holy, acceptable unto God, which is your reasonable service." — Rom. xii. 1.

My previous lectures have been chiefly upon moral subjects. We have considered the duties devolving upon us, in the ordinary relations of life, with reference to our usefulness and happiness in this world. The motives by which the necessity of a good life has been urged, have been drawn, in part, from those considerations of propriety, of self-respect, and even of worldly success, which belong to this life alone, and are in themselves considered motives of expediency, as much as of right. I have, indeed, endeavored to preserve an under current of religious feeling, and thereby impart seriousness and solemnity to our thoughts.

My own mind has never been drawn, even for a moment, from the responsibility under which we stand to God. The truth that the present life is also a preparation for the future, has been continually present to me. Even in those remarks which may have seemed most exclusively prudential and worldly, I have desired to make all rest on this foundation.

If the present life were all of which we have promise, there are, perhaps, sufficient motives to keep a sensible man from the dissipations and wickedness of the world, and to induce him to spend his time in a course of sobriety and usefulness; but it is only when we think of the present life as the childhood of the soul, and that the character which the soul forms for itself here must go with it to the threshold of Eternity, that we can discern the infinite importance of goodness, and the fearfulness of that wrong which we do to our own souls through sin. As we say to the child, to be diligent in his school-days, because upon this his character as a man will depend, so do we say of the present life, that we should spend it well, because we are now educating ourselves for good or evil in the world to come. Is it not a thought to startle us from indifference? Does it not confer sacredness upon the common duties of life, and the brand of deeper infamy upon its sins? If it were only the respectability and the comfort, the rational enjoyment and usefulness of a life which must end in fifty or sixty years, we might almost excuse ourselves in sin, by saying that after all it is a matter of small importance and will soon be over; but when we think of it all, as only the beginning now, the dread consequences of which will be developed in the unknown but never ending future, our hearts are sobered from their folly, our consciences are wakened from their sleep.

I would not urge upon you the fear of hell, as the leading motive to a good life, for I find no authority in Scripture, in the preaching of Christ or his Apostles, for so doing; although they did not conceal the "terrors of the Lord," they used them "for the persuasion of men." They spoke plainly of the terrible consequences of sin, both here and hereafter; but it was chiefly by the beauty of goodness and by the love of God that they made their appeal. "I beseech you therefore, by the mercies of God," said the Apostle, "to present your bodies a living sacrifice, holy, acceptable unto God, which is your reasonable service." The true Christian preaching calls attention to the dreadful consequences of sin, only so far as to make the pursuit of virtue the reasonable service of God. Nothing, I suppose, has contributed more to bring religion into contempt, than the manner in which the fear of hell has been made "the hangman's whip, to keep the world in order." It is sometimes used as a motive, not less mercenary than the most common rewards of virtue in the present life. We may learn to think of heaven and hell as the payment for so much virtue, or the punishment for so much sin, just as we think of money received in payment for work done, or of the jail as the penalty of crime. It is better to conduct ourselves well, even from such motives as these, than not at all; but the motives are certainly of a low kind, and not well calculated to develop a high order of virtue.

If we can love God only so long as the fear of his anger is before us, our case is, at the best, but a bad one. If sin is hateful to us, only because its outward punishment, either here or hereafter, is terrible, our hearts may in fact be loving the sin itself and yearning for its commission all the time. We must rise to a much higher state of feeling than this, before we are properly Evangelical or Gospel Christians. We must learn to feel that virtue is its own exceeding great reward, and that we are paid, over and over again, for all our exertions to do right, for all acts of self-denial, for all perseverance in well-doing, by the character which we are thus giving to our own souls, by the communion which we are thus holding with the pure and good and above all with God himself. We should feel, that in the commission of a base action, or the indulgence of bad passions, the baseness and degradation are themselves the greatest punishment. The hope of heaven then becomes a right and worthy motive, because its reward is in the continuance and perfect completion, through eternity, of that serene delight which begins here. The fear of future retribution then becomes an availing motive, of which we need not be ashamed, because it is chiefly the continuance of that same baseness of character to which sin now degrades us, and by which, as we are separated from God's love now, we have reason to fear that we shall be separated from him more widely hereafter.

Religion ought not to be made the calculation of profit and loss. As the body hungers for its daily food, because needful for its maintenance, so should the soul hunger and thirst after righteousness, because necessary for its full development, for its healthy action, for the maintenance of its real life. As spiritual beings, we live just in proportion to our degree of goodness. When we commit sin, the soul languishes. If it were possible to be completely buried in sin, the soul would die. It finds no elements of life in wickedness, but all its faculties are cramped, its beauty lost, its capacity of improvement impaired. Compare the soul of one whose life has been consecrated to goodness and truth, with that of one whose whole life has been wasted in self-indulgence, or given to the pursuit of sin. When they are both called to the judgment-seat of Christ, how differently do they appear! I do not now say how different must be the judgment pronounced on them, but how different they are in themselves. You would hardly suppose them to be of the same family or kindred. They seem to be of a different nature. Equally different, therefore, must be their destination. The sentence is in themselves already, "Depart from me, ye cursed," or "Come unto me, ye blessed of my Father."

Nothing, however, can be more absurd, than to think of the heavenly life as being, in a meritorious sense, the reward of a good life on earth. The Saviour taught that "when we have done all we are unprofitable servants, doing only what is our duty to do." That is to say, God may properly claim our best service, and therefore we can do nothing to establish a claim upon him in return. We should not speak of future salvation, as if it were a debt due from God to us, to be claimed, just as the aborer claims payment for the work he has done. It is as though you were to confer benefits, day after day, and year after year, upon some one who has no claim upon you, and he should demand the continuance of such benefits as a right. Even if our whole duty were performed, the hope of eternal life must be founded upon the continuance of the Divine goodness, the faithfulness of the Divine promise; but when we confess, as we must, that, instead of our whole duty, not one half has been done, the absurdity of making that imperfect performance a claim to infinite reward is sufficiently evident. To escape punishment for what remains undone, or for what has been done badly, is in itself a great deliverance. Our relation towards God is that of sinners who ask forgiveness, of penitents seeking for pardon. When, therefore, in addition to the forgiveness asked, a life of joy is promised, a life of communion with the just made perfect, with the holy Jesus and with the infinite God himself, our hearts overflow with gratitude, and all thoughts of our own merit are for ever put away.

We know that repentance and a renewed life are made a condition, and they are an indispensable condition, of future happiness. I do not know of any part of Scripture which encourages us to hope for salvation upon any other terms. But the condition on which a benefit is conferred, is very different from its procuring cause. You may promise to a poor man that, if he will come to your house, you will relieve his wants; his coming is therefore a condition, upon the fulfilment of which your assistance will be given; but who would pretend that it is in any proper sense meritorious? The gift would come from your liberality, as much as if no condition had been annexed. Or, if you were to receive a young person as a scholar, with the promise, that, if he uses his advantages well up to a certain point, so as to prepare himself for greater, they shall be given to him; in one sense this would appear as a reward, but the obligation resting upon you would come only from your own promise, and not at all on the ground of his merit. Your promise itself was given gratuitously, and its fulfilment is only the completion of a kindness begun.

So far as the idea of reward is contained in the promise of future bliss, it is contained in the illustration now given. We are placed here, the children of God, surrounded by blessings, with abundant opportunities of improvement, the tokens of God's love everywhere present, and with the promise, that, if we use these present blessings for our own education in goodness and truth, so as to be capable of receiving greater blessings hereafter, they shall be given to us. Use the earth well, and heaven shall be yours. Educate yourselves for the higher life, and you shall enter upon it. Follow God's present guidance, and he will lead you from glory to glory, from one height of excellence and enjoyment to another, through the ages of eternity. If we call the fulfilment of these gracious promises the reward of a Christian life, it is not, in the strict sense of reward, as a debt from nim who gives it, which we can claim on the score of merit, but only on the faithfulness of him by whom the promise is made. It is better to say that the regenerate life is the condition on which salvation is freely offered through Jesus Christ.

And why is it made a condition? Not because God gains any thing by its fulfilment; he requires nothing of us, as though he needed it, "seeing that in him we live and move and have our being." Our best holiness is but the working of his spirit in our hearts, and the part which we do is to submit ourselves to the heavenly guidance. It is made the condition, so far as we can understand the subject, just as each step in knowledge is the condition of further progress. It is imposed upon us, not by an arbitrary decree, but by the law under which we live. "To him that hath shall be given," is the law of spiritual progress. Nothing can be given to those who have not the capacity to receive it. I believe that God always confers upon us the greatest amount of spiritual blessings that we are capable to receive. By using the present gift the capacity enlarges, and the human soul, through the continuance of God's grace, expands to an angel's form. This is eternal life, of which we must have the earnest here, if we would enter upon that greater promise hereafter.

In the same manner, a wrong idea is often entertained of the punishment threatened; as though our sins were a wrong done to God, an injury inflicted upon him, for which he will take vengeance. But the Scriptures say, "He that committeth sin wrongeth his own soul." How can the finite injure the Infinite? How can the creature inflict a wrong upon the Creator, who sustains him in life and gives him the power by which the wrong is done? How can we think of God as thirsting for vengeance against those, whom by a breath he could sweep away for ever? That contest would be too unequal. It is true that the Scripture uses language, a literal interpretation of which would convey this idea of punishment, but a moment's thought shows its true meaning. The explanation of all God's dealing with us, however severe it may be, and of all the threatenings contained in his word, is found in the twofold character of God; first, as our Heavenly Father, and, secondly, as a being infinitely wise and holy.

As a Father, he directs all things for our good, but, leaving to us freedom to obey or disobey him, to use the means of grace or to neglect them, we are of course subject to sin and the ruin it produces. As a Being infinitely wise and holy, our departure from sin and return to goodness is absolutely indispensable to his favor; it is equally indispensable to our own real happiness. Whatever degree of suffering, therefore, may be necessary under God's parental discipline, however terrible it may seem and however terrible it may be, is the inevitable consequence. The moral government of God, in which holiness is made the absolute law, must be maintained. The "terrors of the Lord" therefore sufficiently appear. But there is nothing, in the infliction of his severest sentences, like human vengeance, or the expression of anger as a personal feeling. We do not pretend to interpret all the principles of the Divine government, as though we sat upon the judgment-seat, but the general principles now laid down may be asserted, we think, with the utmost confidence. It is a view of religion, at the same time the most cheering and most alarming we can take. It delivers us from superstitious fears, from slavish trembling before God, while it reveals to us the absolute necessity of a good and holy life. There is no escape from it. It is required not only by the commands of God, but by the nature of God itself. It is required also by our own nature, which is, in this respect, created after the image of God.

It thus appears in what manner the Christian life is the condition of salvation, not as a procuring cause, but as the indispensable preparation. But the question now arises, In what does that preparation consist? What do we mean by a Christian life as a condition of acceptance? This is an important question, and upon its answer our views of practical religion will chiefly depend. The same question was proposed by a prophet in olden time, and his answer will guide us to the truth. "What is it, O man, that the Lord thy God requireth of thee, but this, to do justly, love mercy, and walk humbly with thy God?" It consists, therefore, of two parts; the faithful and kind performance of our duties to each other, and the spirit of devotion towards God. Both parts are equally important, and neither is perfect without the other. The same answer is given by Christ himself, although in different words, when he says that there are but two essential commandments, of which the first is "to love the Lord our God with all the heart," and the second, "to love our neighbor as we love ourselves."

There is a great difference between morality and religion. We may say, indeed, that morality cannot be perfect, without religious principle for its foundation; and as a matter of fact, this is true. Worldly principles are not enough to make a man truly good. But in idea we may consider morality quite abstractly from religion, and in practical life we find many instances of those who are called moral men, and who are so in all the common relations of life, but upon whose hearts the influence of religion has not yet been shed. Worldly and selfish motives are enough to conform our characters to a high standard of respectability, and our natural affections, if well directed in early life, will lead to the practice of those virtues, upon which the comfort of our families and the peace of society depend. Sometimes a degree of excellence is thus attained deserving of great respect. We do not undervalue it. Such obedience is very often, as it is said of the law, "the schoolmaster which brings us to Christ"; but it is evident, even to superficial thought, that, however correct the outward conduct may be, its real character depends upon the motive by which it is actuated. You may describe a man who, to human observation, wrongs no person, but fulfils all his duties with scrupulous exactness, of whom you may yet say that God is not in all his thoughts. You may imagine such an one, we do not say that you will find him in actual life, but you may imagine him to be impelled in all that he does by motives of self-interest. It may all be nothing but a refined calculation of profit and loss. It may be all in the service of the world and from the fear of man. Now, however estimable his exterior may be, and however valuable in the common relations of life, we cannot help admitting that the soul, when actuated by no higher motives than these, is very far from its own highest advancement. Change its ruling principle; let the supreme love of goodness take possession of it, for goodness' sake; infuse into it the martyr's spirit of self-sacrifice; let self-consecration take the place of self-love; let God become the object of supreme worship, instead of the world, and how complete a change in the spiritual nature is produced! It is as complete regeneration as the change from vice to virtue; as complete, we say, and as real, although not as open to outward observation.

Such is an extreme case, but it serves to show the essential difference between morality and religion. The common experience of life shows it equally well, and in a more practical manner. As the world goes, moral men are very frequently not religious men; and what is still more unfortunate, those who claim to be religious are not always moral. This is a manifest and gross inconsistency, and proves that their religion itself is either shallow or hypocritical; but instances of it are not uncommon. Men who have their seasons of fervent prayer, who are carried even beyond the bounds of reason by religious zeal, who make many professions, and that too not without sincerity, are yet sometimes known as men not to be trusted, who will be guilty of overreaching, falsehood, and other offences, which the common morality of life rebukes. The religion of such persons is not always hypocritical, but more frequently shallow. It is founded upon wrong principles. It is the result of wrong education. It comes from the idea that the worship of God is something external, which he requires for his own sake, instead of that "reasonable service," which consists in presenting the body a living sacrifice to him. When we learn that "they who worship God must worship him in spirit and in truth," and that no worship can be acceptable to him which comes from an impure or bigoted heart, or which is accompanied by an impure or dishonest life, then the religion which tries to dispense with morality, and the faith which tries to do without works, wil be abandoned. Religion, if rightly considered, is the spirit in which we live. When we have the spirit of Christ, we have the Christian religion. In proportion as we obtain it we are Christians. It must penetrate and gradually purify our whole nature. It must govern us in all the departments of life. It begins with that fear of God which is the fear to commit sin, and is perfected in that love of God which leads to the love of goodness. It infuses into all our actions a heavenly purpose, and gives to all our steps a heavenward direction. It gradually becomes the ruling motive and gives a new character, almost a higher nature, to the soul. We do not say that this is at once accomplished, but it is the work proposed. It is the tendency which Religion gives to the soul, conforming it to that which is heavenly, raising it above that which is earthly, taking away the selfish life and bringing the life of God into the soul of man. It holds before us the perfect example of Jesus Christ, the Son of God, and, teaching us that we also are the children of God, encourages us to press forward towards the mark of our high calling. It commands us to become like Jesus, and in that one word includes the highest self-devotion to God, and the most careful performance of all the duties of life.

What I would chiefly urge upon you now is the necessity of religion, as a pervading influence of life, to every one of us, especially to those who are young. If there are any whose passions are already subdued under other discipline, they will still need its comforting and purifying presence; but the young cannot dispense with it, without the greatest risk even to their common morality. Religion is needed by them in the development of their faculties, in the education of their minds, in the government of life. It is the balance-wheel, to impart steady and regular action to those impulses, which will otherwise have unequal and destructive power. It is needed to give them consistency of character, to remove them from that strong influence of example which is the ruin of so many, to give them the power of saying NO, when they are tempted. Religion is the highest and strongest principle of self-guidance. It enables one to stand alone, if in a right position; to refuse following the multitude in doing evil. I appeal to young men if they do not need such an influence. Do you not often feel your resolutions giving way, because they have no higher support than your own will? Would it not often be a relief to you when tempted, to think, I cannot do this because my religion forbids me? If that silent appeal were open to you, would it not enable you to escape from many of the false judgments of the world?

I know that young persons are not apt to take this view of the subject. They are more apt to think that religion is intended as a consolation to those who are in trouble; as a refuge to the alarmed and repenting sinner; as a staff to support the declining years of the aged; as the promise which allays the fears of the dying. It is indeed all this, but it is also something more. It is the purifying influence of life, needed by the young, not less than by the old; by the prosperous, not less than by the unfortunate. It is as important to us in the fulness of strength as upon the dying bed.

There are some who think that they may spend the whole of life as they please, in frivolous worldliness or heartless sin; and that at the close of life, or even upon the death-bed, they can make it all right between themselves and God, by a few earnest prayers and by casting themselves upon the merits of Jesus

Christ. How uncertain is such a reliance, even at the best! How can we tell that death may not be so sudden as to give not a day or an hour for preparation? How little opportunity of thought do the days of sickness afford, when the body is tortured by pain, and the mind disturbed from its healthy action, and the anxious faces of friends fill us with anxiety, and our own hearts are trembling because we are not ready to die! But still more, what right have we to expect that God will hear that last despairing cry, of those who through their whole lives have refused to call upon him? We would not extinguish that hope when there is no other; but neither Scripture nor reason justifies us in making it our chief reliance. It is a living sacrifice which God demands, not a dying sacrifice. Under the Jewish law, he who brought a diseased or imperfect offering to the altar, from his herds or flocks, was rebuked and rejected. The offering was required to be without spot or stain. Under the Christian dispensation, shall we do less honor to the God and Father of our Lord Jesus Christ? Shall we give the vigor of our days to worldly and selfish pursuits, and at last come with reluctant steps, with the poor wreck of a decaying body, and offer that to God for his acceptance? There is a meanness in it, a baseness of calculation, from which our hearts revolt. To make Him, who ought to be the first and highest in our thoughts, the last resort of our feebleness, is little short of blasphemy. To acknowledge, as we do, that Christ died to redeem us from sin and death, but deliberately to put him away from our thoughts and refuse obedience to his commands, until all our worldly purposes have been accomplished, and all our sinful appetites indulged, and then turn to him, saying: "Now we will accept thy salvation; now we will rely upon thy merits"; — does not such a hope, even when it comes, border upon despair? What then shall we say of those who hold it before them as their plan of life, and who devote their days to sin, with such an expectation of final escape?

There are some who neglect religion in

their youth, because they think that by and by it will be easier to become religious. They flatter themselves that youthful folly will die out, of itself; that the strength of their passions will become less, and the work of self-government easier; that the temptations of life will not be so many, nor so hard to resist; that as they grow older, religious thought will become more natural to them, and worldliness less attractive. They hope, therefore, to grow into religion by the natural progress of life. In other words, starting in a wrong direction, and travelling as fast as they well can, they expect to arrive at the right conclusion of their journey. The whole experience of life shows their folly. When did you ever know bad passions to become less by indulgence? When did wrong habits ever correct themselves, or become easier of correction by continuance? You say that it is hard for you to be religious now; I grant it. It will require your best exertions and the assistance of God's spirit, which he has also promised. But it will be harder next year, and every year that you live, until it becomes almost impossible. Begin the work now, enlist the power of habit on the side of virtue, make religion the ruling principle, and you will then find that as you grow older the work will become easier. Walking in a right direction, surmounting one obstacle after another, although you may seem to progress slowly, yet every step is so much gained, and your whole life will accomplish a great deal. Then, at the close of life, you may cast yourself upon the mercy of God, of which you will still have enough need, with a reasonable hope, yea, with a strong confidence, that his promise of salvation through Jesus Christ will be fulfilled.

But there are some, who admit all I have now said, but upon whom it has no practical influence. They admit that religion is the strongest influence that can be brought to bear upon them. They admit its absolute necessity; they do not believe in a death-bed repentance; yet they remain irreligious, and do not even put themselves under religious instruction. And this, not from a determinate purpose to neglect religion, but for reasons which are scarcely reasons at all. Perhaps it is only from a habit of procrastination. Some decided step is needed in the beginning, some change in their ordinary mode of life; and as there seems to be no necessity for beginning to-day, they wait until to-morrow; until gradually the intention itself dies away, and the habits of irreligion become confirmed.

I have also known many persons, who have suffered the better part of life to pass without placing themselves under religious influences, because they have not quite determined what church to attend. Their religious opinions are not fixed. They visit sometimes one place of worship and sometimes another, or, in the doubt where to go, do not go anywhere; so that their thoughts become scattered, the regularity of habit is broken up, their opinions, instead of becoming more settled, are more wavering, and the result is complete indifference or scepticism. Let me, therefore, in conclusion, say a few words upon this subject. I cannot properly now enter upon a discussion of religious doctrines, nor do any thing to settle your minds concerning them. For I can honestly say, that I have had no sectarian purpose to accomplish in these lectures. It is a matter of secondary importance to me, whether those who have heard them are led to make this their place of worship, or some other. If they are awakened to the necessity of religion and encouraged in the practice of virtue, I shall be abundantly content. But I may take the liberty of advising every young man to select some place of public worship as his own, and to occupy his seat there as regularly as the Sunday comes. I do not mean that he should never go to any church but his own, for it is useful at times to go elsewhere, to keep him from becoming narrow-minded and bigoted. But he should have his own customary place of worship, where he will attend, unless sufficient reason leads him for the time to some other.

He will soon find his account in this. It is not that a single sermon, or many sermons, will do him much good. Sermons are very often dull; the subjects treated are often such as do not interest the young, and the hour spent at church will sometimes be the longest in the day. You may think that you would have done better to stay at home and read, and so far as mere instruction is concerned this will sometimes be true. But the general influence of the House of Prayer is, nevertheless, in the highest degree beneficial. I am disposed to think it almost indispensable, as a means of religious improvement. You will find very few persons who neglect it without injury to themselves. It is not so much the instruction imparted, although that is something, but a higher direction is given to the thoughts; the eager pursuit of worldly things is moderated; our sins are rebuked, if not by the sermon, yet by the Scripture read and the prayers offered; we are reminded of many things which, although we know them well enough, we are prone to forget; above all, we hear the name of Jesus Christ as our Saviour, and of the Infinite God as our Heavenly Father, and as our hearts respond, in unison with many others, to those blessed words, which are more dear to us as they become more familiar, the united influence of our own prayers, and of sympathy with those around us, and of all the associations of the place, excites within us a yearning after goodness, and turns us from the love of sin. We go away self-rebuked, yet encouraged for new endeavor. We have found consolation under sorrow, strength to resist temptation, and perhaps the hope of eternal life. Such is the natural and proper influence of the place where prayer is wont to be made. We shall not fail to experience it, if we are truly engaged in the work of self-improvement, in the formation of the Christian character. We do not speak of church-going as a meritorious act, in itself considered; but as a judicious act, which, when done with a right motive, is almost sure to produce a good result. Its neglect leaves the Sunday unoccupied, and opens the way to many temptations. The religious instruction of our childhood is gradually forgotten. We become more worldly-minded and less devout;

the associations both of the Sunday and of the week-day become less favorable to virtue, and at the end of a few years we find abundant reason to lament that we ever departed from the habits of our early days.

If, then, it is wise to attend regularly at some church, upon what principles shall we make the selection? We answer, go where you hear the Gospel most faithfully preached, and where you feel the influence upon your own character to be the best. Compare the preaching you hear with the Bible you read. "Judge for yourselves what is right," according to this standard, and you are not likely to go far wrong. Among all the different creeds taught, you may not be able to decide which is absolutely correct, and there are many points of doctrine concerning which you may always remain in doubt; but the great principles of Christianity are plain enough to all. With regard to its leading doctrines, also, you may without much difficulty form an opinion. But above all, and what is most important, you will have no difficulty in deciding where you are most benefited, and that is your proper place of worship.

Wherever it may be, may the God of peace go with you! I have sought to do my own duty towards you as a minister of Jesus Christ, and, if I have spoken too plainly, have endeavored to "speak the truth in love." I end, therefore, as I began, — "beseeching you, by the mercies of God, to present your bodies a LIVING SACRIFICE, holy, acceptable unto God, which is your reasonable service."

THE END.

www.ingramcontent.com/pod-product-compliance
Lightning Source LLC
LaVergne TN
LVHW011225110826
845150LV00006B/1553

9781425515324